Stop My Crisis:

Be the 1 in 5

How to Keep YOUR Business From Failing!

The Business Owner's & Sales Professional's Guide to Success

By

Vivian C. Gaspar

The content within this book is not intended to take the place of a consultation with a qualified professional regarding the readers' specific circumstances.

This book's ISBN categories are:
Finance, Business, Self-Help Technique

Published by Carpe 28, LLC.
Succasunna, New Jersey

2015 Copyright Pending

No part of this book may be reproduced without written consent.

Copyright © 2015 Carpe 28, LLC

All rights reserved.

ISBN: 978-0-9832121-1-9   51982

DEDICATION

This book, and all my dreams of helping as many people as possible through education on a broad variety of topics, is due to my love for the people closest to me. I actually had always attributed my entrepreneurial spirit to my father, who had always been an inspiration as I saw him try his hand at many businesses ever since I was young and throughout my adulthood. My mother had always drempt I would come a writer. Therefore, I am quite happy to say that this book as well as it's sister book, "Stop My Crisis – Facing Life's Challenges Head on", can be attributed to both my parents, whom I love deeply.

I would also like to dedicate this book to Richard Frantz, who has been the single most influential individual in my adult life and has always been very supportive of my entrepreneurial endeavors, including this book series.

Also, I am also very appreciative and grateful to have worked with V. James Castiglia in the mortgage modification arena. I not only appreciate Jim Castiglia's hard work and dedication to his clients, but I also really enjoyed learning from him in the countless client meetings I had the privilege to witness. Mr. Castiglia's broad knowledge base and his manner of delivering that knowledge in a comforting and tireless fashion is always an inspiration to me; I felt driven in my work because of it. Without Mr. Castiglia and my experiences working for and with him and his exceptional staff, this book would never have been possible. Thank you, Jim!

Vivian C. Gaspar

Contents

Dedication iii

Foreword viiii

Acknowledgements x

THE BACKBONE OF YOUR BUSINESS

Chapter 1: You Are Not Your Business Card
By Ted Fattoross 11

Chapter 2: What Form of Business Should I Set Up?
By V. James Castiglia, Esq. 14

Chapter 3: The Power and Value of Your Business Plan
By Jack M. Bleiberg, CPA 20

Chapter 4: Insurances Every Business Owner Must Have
By Terrence P. Coughlin, CPCU, ARM, AICA 25

Chapter 5: Risk Awareness
By Raffi Jamgotchian... 28

Chapter 6: Tips in Renting or Buying Commercial Real Estate
By Helene Strumeyer 37

Chapter 7: Life and Health Insurance for The Business Owner
By Harry Herbst 40

Chapter 8: Goal Setting: Obtain Your Business Objectives
By Arnold Rintzler, Certified Business Coach 42

Chapter 9: Time Management: We All Get The Same 24 Hours In a Day - Learn The Secrets to Making The Most of Your Time
By Arnold Rintzler, Certified Business Coach 58

MONEY: GETTING AND KEEPING MORE OF IT

Chapter 10 Merchant Services: Understanding The Costs and Uses To Getting New Clients
By Vivian C. Gaspar and Frank Gallipoli 67

Chapter 11: Cash-Flow Tips for Your Business
By Vito Mazza 71

Chapter 12: Alternative Business Financing: Bridge Your Financial Gap
By Vivian C. Gaspar and Frank Gallipoli 76

Chapter 13: Getting Paid Promptly In The Construction Business
By Douglas A. Goldstein, Esq. 79

Chapter 14: 3 Attributes Your Next Financial Advisor Must Have
By Brian T. Cody, CFP 81

THE LEGAL NECESSITIES

Chapter 15: Mediation for Business Owners
By Robert J. McDonnell, MS APM 83

Chapter 16: Employment Law Facts
By Marc Garbar, Esq. 88

Chapter 17: New Jersey's Consumer Fraud Act: What Is a Consumer?
By Douglas A. Goldstein, Esq. 97

Chapter 18: Being Preferred Is Not Always a Good Thing
By Douglas A. Goldstein, Esq. 99

EMPLOYEES - HOW TO GET AND KEEP THE RIGHT PEOPLE BEHIND YOU

Chapter 19: Vision, Leadership, and Strategy: Along the Path to Building Your Business Success
By Donna Price 102

Chapter 20: W2 or 1099? The Wrong Choice Can Cost You Your Business
By James Hyland 108

Chapter 21: Should I Hire an Intern?
By Michele J. Alexander, B.A., CP 111

Chapter 22: Background Investigations
By Eric B. Segal 114

Chapter 23: 18 Questions to Your Next Right Hire
By Joanne Lucas 118

Chapter 24: Seven Techniques Employers Can Employ To Keep Employees Happy
By Brian T. Cody, CFP... 122

Chapter 25: Low to No-Cost Benefits to Attract and Retain Employees
By Katherine Woodfield Hermes 124

Chapter 26: Medical Care Discount Plans: An Affordable Alternative to Health Insurance
By Ciro J. Giue 130

MARKETING AND SALES FOR YOU AND YOUR BUSINESS

Chapter 27: You Are Not Your Company
By S.E. Day 133

Chapter 28: In-Person Business Networking
By Josh Dill 146

Chapter 29: Public Speaking Skills for Business Owners and Sales Professionals
By Marlene J. Waldock 150

Chapter 30: Practical Marketing for Every Business Budget
By Ronald Hatcher 153

Chapter 31: General Selling Skills
By Paul L. Morris 164

Chapter 32: Cold Calling Tips for Business Owners and Sales Professionals
By Deborah Anderson 179

Chapter 33: How to Use Social Media to Boost Your Business
By Marie Griffin 181

Chapter 34: Five LinkedIn Tricks To Double Your Sales
By Julbert Abraham 192

RIDING THE ROUGH TIMES

Chapter 35: Bookkeeping Tips to Save You Stress
By Rose Benson 195

Chapter 36: Getting Your Business to Survive Tough Economies
By Neil Pinkman 204

Chapter 37: Create a "Get Off Your A$$" Mindset
By Sean Carroll 209

Chapter 38: Psychological Tips for the Entrepreneur to Stay the Course Through Tough Times
By Rich Dowling, MA, LPC, MAC 219

Chapter 39: Should You Throw in the Towel? Evaluate Current Status, Growth History, and Growth Potential
By Donna Price 224

Chapter 40: 10 Ideas for Your Next Business Startup
By Vivian C. Gaspar 229

About the Contributing Authors 231

Foreword

As someone who has worked individually in the last two years with over 300 families in financial crisis as the Public Relations Director and Mortgage Modification Specialist with the legal office of V. James Castiglia in New Jersey, I found myself hearing similar stories and repeatedly giving the same advice. In addition to assisting couples with the proper completion of mortgage modification applications, I also gave advice on a range of topics where I had developed expertise. My experience includes owning a marketing company, being a recruiter, and helping people decipher their current mortgages; mortgage loan officer and now alternative lending specialist.

One of my responsibilities as Mr. Castiglia's Public Relations Director was to give speeches to civic organizations, such as the Lions Club and Rotary Club, at their locations in New Jersey, as well as the Department of Labor, public libraries, and The Learning Annex. After many of these speeches, during which I would educate the members of these clubs, I was approached to spread my information to a wider audience and to consider writing a book.

In February of 2010, I started to give the idea of writing a book on mortgage modification and the foreclosure process more serious consideration. However, I wanted to have a wider impact. As I gave this idea more thought, I concluded that I could help a wider base of people in crisis if I covered a broad subject base. As I started an outline of chapters and topics I wanted to see included in my book, I immediately thought of all the business contacts I had accumulated over the years. This book is my opportunity to bring to you the knowledge of seasoned professionals on specific topics where they have great expertise.

For many years now I have educated people on topics ranging from "Mortgage Trivia for Everyone" and "Identity Theft and Understanding the Basics of Credit Scores" to "Understanding Mortgage Modification and the Foreclosure Process." Now I want to bring to people the most concisely worded information on a variety of the most critical financial survival topics which everyone can use at one low price.

Please enjoy the journey of learning contained within the following pages, and please e-mail me at Vivian@StopMyCrisis.com telling me how the information in this book has helped to improve your life.

Thank you, and happy reading!

Vivian C. Gaspar

Acknowledgements

As the creator of this reference book, I would like to take the time to express my gratitude to the 31 professionals without whom this book could never have come to fruition.

First and foremost, I really want to acknowledge and thank my parents. Thanks also to Richard Frantz, my editor and closest companion of the last 26 years, who has been instrumental in my being able to bring this book to its completion. It has been an ongoing challenge to support the time and energy that I needed to devote to this project.

I am extremely grateful to the 31 authors who were very generous with their time and sharing their expertise. I believe that these gracious individuals should be commended for their generosity, since all of them have very busy professional practices.

Another critical member of my team is Jim Castiglia, who is my staff attorney and contributing co-author on several chapters and the reason for this book's very existence.

Vivian C. Gaspar

Chapter 1

You Are Not Your Business Card

By Ted Fattoross

"Carpe Diem!"
-Unknown

You are not your business card. You are a person. Attending a networking function can be a little like dating. When you go out on a first date, would you propose marriage before even ordering your meal? Yet, for some reason that is exactly what we do — at both social and business networking events. We are not our business cards. Some people have the notion that once cards are exchanged, this ritual is a rite of passage allowing one to do or say anything. In truth, it's just a small piece of paper – smaller than a credit card – and has a street value of about a nickel. It's who we are that really matters, not what we do. It's the size of our heart, not our business card, that's important. It's what we stand for, not what we sell, that's relevant. It's who we associate with that defines us, not where we live or what we drive. It's why we do what we do that really counts. You are not your job – you are Infinite Opportunities, Unlimited Dreams and Ageless Beauty. We are not sharks in suits, we are eagles with wings.

Who am I? Just a guy, who woke up at 4:00 this morning and realized that most of us have been hypnotized at an early age and as adults have remained in this hypnotic state. For good reason we were taught not to talk to strangers. So we paid attention, became cautious, less curious. Locked our doors and closed our minds; put on the armor of the "right business suit." Went out and got business cards and communicated by phone and email – yes, even to the people sitting in the same room – both at home and at the office.

The wakeup call? We are not children – we can talk to strangers. We can get to know the person at the check-out line, the bus, the train, the plane and bagel shop. We are not our business cards. We are people. People do not do business with business cards, they do business with people. So, maybe the real question is not what type, style, or color should I use on my business card. Maybe the real question is: Who am I? And what do I stand for – and why do I do what I do? By the way, these questions are frightening – terrifying. But these are the real questions, the real deal. Are you the real deal? Too many people follow what I call the "family of origin script" and live a life not their own. Living the "family of origin script" is comfortable, safe, and secure. In truth, it's a prison – three "hots and a cot" as they say behind bars. Safe. Leaving this place takes courage. Courage is not being fearless; courage is moving forward while facing our fear, period. Our real fear is not of failure. Our real fear is of possibility. Of what we are, of what we may become. Our real fear is that glimpse of amazing abundance, infinite wisdom, and boundless possibilities. We fear ourselves, our possibilities. Within each of us is a seed. A seed that must be planted, nurtured, cultivated, and embraced. It's our seed – not mom's, dad's, our teachers', preacher's, or neighbor's. We own it and are responsible for its outcome. We own the outcome. We allow others to direct, dictate, and manage us in an all-out effort not to take ownership of our lives, thus avoiding the ownership of the outcome. We lose by default no matter how large our portfolio, value of our estate, or size of our business. Never live by default. Own your seed, own your journey, and celebrate the ownership of your outcome. Remind yourself that every day above ground is a great one – a gift, be thankful. Rejoice in all things. Please read the following poem I gave birth to when I first started my journey of sowing my seed. For the record, since then, I have not used a business card, yet have completed over 6000 speaking events, over 100 consulting assignments, and counseled over 1,000,000 people. I am not my business card, I am Infinite Opportunities, Unlimited Dreams, and Boundless Energy, who is inspired not only by the universe but by its Master Artist – the Creator. Here is my poem - enjoy!

We are born complete,

we are not born deficient.

We need not be fixed,

for we are not broken.

We are whole, not fragmented.

We need to nurture the child in us,

not force it to grow up.

We are love, only love.

It is fear that prevents us from

being who we really are.

We are love, only love.

-Ted Fattoross

P.S.: The greatest gift I am thankful for is the honor, the privilege, and the joy of being the daddy of Taylor and Jared Fattoross

Carpe Diem
Ted Fattoross
CEO/Founder
Joinnetworkplus.com
TedSpeak.com
Educational Services
Safe School Foundation
Ebony/Ivory

Chapter 2

What Form of Business Should I Set Up?

By V. James Castiglia, Esq.

While there are several different types of business organizations (depending on the state you live in), it is important to remember that for income tax purposes, there are only two taxpaying entities – individuals and corporations. An individual is a person, and a corporation is a legal person. Although there are more than two forms of business organizations, all of these different types of organizations pay income tax either by:

1. a schedule attached to an individual's income tax return (Federal 1040); or

2. by a corporate income tax return (Federal 1120). The type of business organization you should choose depends on the following factors:

   a) How much personal liability for the business do you want to incur?

   b) What is the amount and type of your start-up capital? For example, is anyone else contributing to the business's startup capital?

   c) How do you want to pay your income taxes?

   d) How easily do you want to set up and operate?

e) How many employees will you have (besides yourself)?

f) What are your plans for long-term succession? For example, who is going to run the business if you die or retire?

The information contained herein is meant to serve as a guide to making your decision and should not take the place of the advice of your own attorney or accountant.

THE SOLE PROPRIETORSHIP

A sole proprietorship is run under your own name and social security number. Usually no state filing is required unless you use a trade name, in which case you will have to file a trade name certificate. The business continues until you stop doing business or you die. You have total and unlimited personal liability for the business debts and obligations. You have full control and management of the business and its operations. It is not a taxable entity; you pay taxes by filing a Schedule C to your personal income tax return. All of the business profits and losses are passed along to you.

THE PARTNERSHIP

A partnership is an agreement between two or more parties and is owned and operated equally by the partners. No state filing is usually required. The business continues until a partner withdraws, retires, or dies. Each partner is jointly and severally liable (fully liable) for the business debts and obligations. The partners share equally the control and management of the business equally (unless you agree in writing to different shares). It is not a taxable entity; you file a Federal Partnership return (1065), but this is an informational return. A Schedule K-1 is then attached to your personal income tax return. All of the business profits and losses are passed along to the partners.

THE LIMITED PARTNERSHIP OR LIMITED LIABILITY PARTNERSHIP

These are variations on a partnership in which limited partners do not have unlimited liability for the debts and obligations of the business, but also do not have a share in the control and management of the business. The New York Yankees is probably the best known limited partnership in the United States; limited liability partnerships are usually for the practice of professional services, e.g., legal or accounting. The formation of these types of businesses is beyond the scope of this chapter and you should consult your legal or accounting professional.

THE CORPORATION

A corporation is formed by a filing with a state government. It is owned by its stockholders, and you can have different classes of stock. A corporation continues perpetually. Stockholders are not liable for the debts and obligations of the corporation – a corporation is (in legal contemplation) a separate person and its own taxpaying entity. Shareholders elect the Directors of the corporation, who in turn hire or appoint the Officers of the corporation, who control and manage the business. In a corporation where only one or a few people own the stock, these people usually fill all of these roles: stockholder, director, and officer. It does not pass through profits and losses to its owners; the corporation pays its own income taxes. It can distribute profits to its shareholders only as dividends. However, those dividends are then taxable again to the shareholder as income. In other words, the profits of a corporation are subject to double taxation in order to get them to the shareholder. Some states (New Jersey) impose a minimum corporate income tax even if the business has no income.

THE S-CORPORATION

An S-corporation is a special type of corporation for companies with limited shareholders. In most states, it has been made obsolete by the existence of Limited Liability Companies. You should consult a professional for advice on an S-Corporation.

THE LIMITED LIABILITY COMPANY

A limited liability company (LLC) is formed by filing with a state government. It is owned by its members. The members are not liable for the debts and obligations of the business. An LLC can be perpetual. Management is determined by an

Operating Agreement between the members. It is not a taxable entity, and profits and losses are usually passed through to the members for inclusion on their individual tax returns.

The Limited Liability Company is a hybrid cross between a sole proprietorship and a Corporation, offering owners direct control over the business with the protection from liability. Today it is the most common and preferred form of business ownership.

ADVANTAGES AND DISADVANTAGES

There are advantages and disadvantages to any of the forms of business ownership. The following charts compare the advantages and disadvantages of an LLC with a sole proprietorship, a partnership, and a corporation.

Advantages of an LLC vs. a Sole Proprietorship

LLC	Sole Proprietorship
• Limited liability for all members easier/less complicated to form • Can possess corporate management structure • Can exist indefinitely; one member or multiple members • Can be taxed under any classification	• Easier/less complicated to form • Easier/less complicated to manage/operate • No statutory requirements • Well-established case law • Always taxed as a sole proprietorship

Disadvantages of an LLC vs. a Sole Proprietorship

LLC	Sole Proprietorship
• Government filing required to form and terminate • May be taxed as a corporation • Inherent rights and duties among members unknown • Piercing the LLC veil • Limited case law and history	• Owner is personally liable • Cannot exist indefinitely • Cannot have more than one owner

Advantages of an LLC vs. a Partnership

LLC	Partnership
• Limited liability for all members • Can possess corporate management structure • Can exist indefinitely • Can have only one member • Easier to qualify for tax flow through treatment	• Easier/less complicated to form and terminate • More flexible in structure and organization • Fewer, if any, statutory requirements • Well-established case law and history

Disadvantages of an LLC vs. a Partnership

LLC	Partnership
• Government filing required to form and terminate • May be taxed as a corporation (federal and state) • Inherent rights and duties among members unknown • Piercing the LLC veil • Limited case law and history	• Can be formed contrary to intention of parties • All partners are jointly and severally liable for partnership debts • Fiduciary duties exist among partners • Can be terminated contrary to intention of partners • Cannot exist indefinitely • Cannot have one-person partnerships

Chapter 3

The Power and Value of Your Business Plan

By Jack M. Bleiberg, CPA

What is a Business Plan?

A business plan is a targeted communication of your vision. Moreover, a written business plan allows you the advantage of creating strategies that are well thought out and provide advanced notice of changes that may be needed at certain milestones. For a growing company, these changes can be for requirements such as financing, additions to staff and facilities, new layers of management, delegation of duties, etc. Even a company that is contracting in size must similarly consider when to release staff and find smaller space.

For the purpose of this chapter, I will refer to growing companies. However, please bear in mind that most companies have slow periods, and even contracting companies need to prepare for these changes in order to survive.

An entity should always have multiple levels of plans. For example: one for the most likely future, one for a greater growth, and one for a lesser result. This allows management to have a guideline as to when and what actions must be taken given the actual circumstances. If there is more than one decision maker, then changes according to the plan can be done without convening the group. If there is only one decision maker, that person can know that they can be gone for a period of time and their plans would be available to designated individuals (wouldn't it be nice to know that you can go on a longer vacation?). An important extension of this thought is that the plan can be used to communicate expectations and goals to your team.

There can be several "targets" of a business plan. The target is that person or group to whom the plan is being presented. Each target has its own unique concerns that must be addressed. So, in addition to the three planning levels described above, there should be iterations for specific users. The more common targets are:

- Internal: This is referred to as the "Strategic Plan." It is a deep consideration of where the corporate vision will go over time and how you plan to make it happen. This is the core business plan and will be our primary objective.

- Financing: Most lenders require a summary plan to support a loan application. In it, you must explain the use of proceeds and how it will be repaid. They must know that their risks are covered.

- Investors: To attract new capital business plans are crucial. In many ways, the considerations are the same as the Financing plan but also add the considerations of the return on investment and an exit plan for the investors.

- Talent Acquisition: Aspects of the plan may be used to attract new key staff members. They should not have access to all information but they should be made excited by the vision and the part they will play.

- Spouse/Family: Never forget your spouse, family, or significant other. You will be expending a lot of effort, passion, and time on your company and possibly dedicating capital. You need to get them "aboard." By sharing your plans with them they will feel a part of it, will understand what you are saying if you bring home success stories and frustrations, and they might even have a good idea that you have not yet considered. Again, too much information is not good. Unless that person is a partner or on your management team, consider sharing only the dream and the highlights. But it is always better to include them in some way.

Basic questions to be answered:

- WHAT service or product does your business offer? What services or products are you considering to add/drop?

- WHY is there a demand for your product or service? Why would you be chosen over a competitor?

- WHO are the key people in your company? What is their business/professional history, education, and industry background? Why are they special to this entity?

- WHERE is the demand? Is it geographic, demographic, etc.?

- WHEN will the plan be executed? What is the timeframe to start and complete? This may be as simple as a generic three year forecast with no specific projects in mind.

Most people think of a business plan as a mathematical / accounting exercise amounting to pages of spreadsheets. This is only a small part of it. Remember, the full plan is the communication of your vision. It needs to be largely narrative and graphics are great. The compulsory numbers are typically at the end and they serve to quantify your thoughts and to establish milestones (timeframe and amounts).

Minimally, the plan should include sections on:

- Marketing and Sales – how are you going to get knowledge of your products and services to your market. Then, how are you going to follow up and get the sale?
- Personnel – What skills do you need to execute the business plan? How available are these people and do you have any at your disposal? If not, how will you attract and retain good employees?

- Risk Management – This is a new hot button. Risk management includes identifying the risks of loss of physical and information assets and the safeguarding and insuring of those risks.
- Legal and Compliance – In our litigious society, how will the company minimize its risk from lawsuits by customers, staff, and competitors. How will we accomplish legal compliance, if appropriate.
- Financial – For internal plans, these analyses should be as detailed as practicable. For external plans, they should be summarized and rounded. Double-check the math! The schedules should include:
    - Use of proceeds if this is for financing or investors.
    - Cash flow over the time period usually by month.
    - Anticipated profit (loss) over the time period usually by month (Return on Investment).
    - Exit plan – the repayment of debt or investment.

Methodology:

- Whatever you are comfortable using is fine so long as it is not a distraction to the process. It is critical that you think clearly and freely. Even if you write it manually and have it beautified later make sure that your thoughts can flow unimpeded.
- Collaborative tools and techniques are the best approach. Try to never do a business plan on your own. We all tend to have "tunnel vision" and we need others to make sure that a realistic expression of your ideas is presented. If you are a sole proprietor, enlist a trusted friend, mentor, or your accountant to be a sounding board for this.
- Software products have been specifically designed for creating business plans. But, they can be pricey. The basics, such as Microsoft's Excel and Word, are popular and are sufficient. There are templates available on the internet.
- Consider that the plan must be easy to update over time. No one can see the future precisely and you will need to update your plan frequently.

- Remember, methodology is the only tool. Do not obsess on it.

Three Do's and Three Don'ts:

DO: Make the effort to create at least the strategic plan.

DO: Make periodic updates to it so that if the business does better or worse you will be prepared.

DO: Enlist all of your partners and / or management to participate. If you have none, find a mentor.

DON'T: Go through all of this effort and never look at it again! Plan to compare actual results to the plan at least quarterly. Use this analysis to understand variances and adjust the future plan.

DON'T: Be discouraged if reality is different that the plan. Take corrective action quickly. A benefit of this work is that you will be able to recognize aberrations quickly and adjust accordingly. No Surprises!

DON'T: Keep this a secret. It is important to communicate your vision to the other involved players such as management, your accountant and attorney, key consultants (as appropriate), and your spouse.

Chapter 4

Insurances Every Business Owner Must Have

By Terrence P. Coughlin, CPCU, ARM, AICA

Any business owner or those contemplating going into business must have a solid risk management strategy that incorporates how they are going to handle various types of risk. Many risk management plans incorporate the use of insurance. Insurance is a tool of the risk manager used to transfer risk to the carrier in the event of an adverse experience or event.

Any size business, including anyone who is either a direct sales representative or has formed any type of legal corporate entity, must have the following insurance:

1. **Property insurance (including renters):** Consists of real property and business owned content. Be sure to maintain adequate property insurance coverage for the things you or your business own. Examine leases - your landlord may require either fire, legal, or tenant legal liability insurance which protect his real property in case your negligence causes damage.

2. **Commercial liability:** Protects the business and its employees in the event of someone being injured or harmed in any way, anywhere it conducts business. Commercial Liability insurance is broken down into several parts.

Per-Occurrence is the most coverage the policy will afford for any one occurrence.

General Aggregate or total amount of insurance which will be afforded under the policy. Many policies can give per occurrence, i.e., 1 million per occurrence and 2 million for the total aggregate of the policy. This can possibly be insufficient for potential lawsuits. This is where umbrella / excess policies are useful.

Products & Completed Operations If your product or service is a likely source of claims, many carriers will use this to limit your claim. For example: If your company produces hammers and the shaft of the hammer is likely to fail or break after repeated use, you can theoretically be sued for each occurrence thus having multiple claims filed against you. This type of policy is designed for third party use of the product after the product has been completed and if the product was found to contain a design flaw.

Professional Services/"Errors & Omissions" aka "E&O" This type of insurance protects various types of professionals from negligence claims by clients and subsequent awards in a lawsuit in the event that the professional mistakenly 'errs' or omits in the performance of their duty. E&O coverage will often cover defense costs but not criminal prosecution nor potential liabilities under civil law. Each policy will contain terms specific to the professional or industry that is covered.

3. **Commercial Auto:** Even if you do not have a corporately owned vehicle you still need auto insurance. Many people assume that a company's auto insurance only applies to the vehicles the company owns. This is completely wrong. One of the more likely sources of litigation a company might have is the liability if you are in a car on company business and have a car accident. The business entity may be sued regardless of who owns the vehicle. Personal Insurance may protect the driver but will not extend to the corporate entity. Businesses need to procure "Non-owned and hired auto liability". This is to protect the entity when an employee is driving a personal vehicle for business purposes and may be purchased one of two ways: If the entity owns vehicles, it can be included on the corporate auto policy or attached to general liability coverage

section. If any company entity owns the vehicle, then they must insure it under the business's name. This can be the number one source of exposure since it is more likely and extremely low cost.

4. **Workman's Compensation**: This policy is meant to protect the worker not the business. All workman's compensation claims are set by the state in which the individual is working. Even if you have no employees many states still require you to purchase workman's compensation insurance. This can cover anyone you have contracted to work with you. You can be covered as a business owner or you can opt in.

5. **Umbrella/Excess Policies:** Umbrella coverage offers protection in the event that the general liability coverage limits do not adequately protect the business owner. This coverage can be sold separately or in conjunction with other types of policies and will depend on how you are buying it and from whom. Remember: these are the minimum coverages in the broadest of terms for the details which are best suited for you and your business. Please contact a local insurance professional for further information.

Chapter 5

Risk Awareness

By Raffi Jamgotchian

"You take the blue pill - the story ends, you wake up in your bed and believe whatever you want to believe. You take the red pill - you stay in Wonderland and I show you how deep the rabbit-hole goes."

-Morpheus from <u>The Matrix</u> (1999)

Risk awareness is an eye-opening experience. It is equal parts enlightening and frightening. Ignorance of the risks around you may be bliss; however, awareness of the risks around you will provide you greater control of your business and the threats that potentially may affect it.

In your capacity of a business owner, you should be aware of the risks to your IT systems. Most business owners don't realize that the activities or behavior that they allow for themselves and their employees bring any risk to their business. Michael Santarcangelo explains in his book, <u>Into the Breach</u> (Santarcangelo, 2008), that most employees are not mindful of the connection between their actions and the consequences of those actions. Santarcangelo continues to say that most employees want to do the right thing; however, they are disconnected between their behavior and its potential effects. If employees are educated of the risks and the consequences of their actions, they will be better stewards of your systems and the data they hold.

Most small businesses do not have written policies on the usage of their systems. In addition, they may allow employees to use the Internet without restriction. Not placing proper limits on employee Internet usage may expose your organization to threats whether it's through websites that aren't appropriate for the business environment, too much information on social network sites, access to their personal email accounts, consumer "drop box" file sharing, or other websites that may have vulnerabilities.

For example, a business may allow employees to visit non-work related websites during off-hours or break-time as long as it's "safe for work." The view here is that management does not see it as a loss of productivity and the computer and Internet connection is not widely used during these times for work-related activities. During a lunch-break, an employee may decide to play some online games. The game website may have some malicious software installed masquerading as a game (the site operators may not even realize it's there!) Now your employee's computer is infected. The next time he fires up your client database or health records, that information could be sent offsite to the attacker's servers for later use. A common misconception is that having a firewall in place and/or antivirus is enough to combat this. Unfortunately, it is not the case. Internet usage policies should reflect these potential risks based on your tolerance.

> ### Pragmatic Solution
>
> Firewalls have come a long way for small and medium businesses. Today's products have added other functions to their capabilities beyond the traditional firewall. These Unified Threat Management or UTM appliances provide a pragmatic way to layer on other security functions. Although each function may not be "best of breed," its practicality outweigh the concerns. By adding on content filtering, based on your company's security or Internet usage policy, or anti-virus filtering at the firewall's edge, you add an additional layer of security in an existing device. The caveat is that it's very tempting to turn on all of the available security functions which can cause slowness to your employees and lower productivity. If your business doesn't require it, don't turn it on.

Passwords are the least expensive way to keep people out of systems they should not have access to. Unfortunately, most companies do not properly set password policies to prevent the use of weak passwords such as dictionary words or information about the person that can be simply found by doing a couple of Internet searches or looking at social networking sites.

The flip side of the password issue is that if you force employees to select very complex passwords that are difficult to remember, they will write them down on those yellow sticky notes and stick them to their monitor or under their keyboards. Security professionals that do security assessments and penetration tests, call these "yellow gold." By checking dumpsters or waste baskets for these sticky notes, an attacker will gain knowledge to your password patterns.

Pragmatic Solution

Ok, so if you can't select weak passwords and you shouldn't select complex passwords because employees will write them down, what should you do? What is a good password? Armstrong and Simonson state the obvious: "a good password is easy to remember but hard to guess." (Armstrong, 1996) One effective method would be to use a pass phrase. Perhaps a line from your favorite movie: "I made him an offer he can't refuse." If your systems or application cannot support long passwords, use the first letter of each word: "Imhaohcr". You can make this further complex by replacing certain letters with similarly looking symbols or numerals: "!mh@0hcr". This makes it something easy to remember but hard to guess.

A password is a one factor authentication system in that it uses something you know, your password. A two factor authentication system adds a second factor to reduce your exposure. A second factor can be something you have like a token that generates one time passwords or something you are like a finger-print, iris, retina scan, face recognition, etc. You must decide as a business owner if the additional expense of adding such a system to protect your assets is worth it. But if it can prevent a loss of customer data it may well be worth the expense.

E-mail has become a critical business tool and has surpassed the phone and fax as the primary method of communication. E-mail has also become a primary method of attack. Spam or unsolicited e-mails are not only annoying and time consuming but they've become more dangerous to your personal privacy and the security of your computer. Millions of computer users are getting infected, spoofed, and tricked by spam e-mails every year forcing the user to pay hefty fees to clean and restore their PCs back to working order.

There are 3 dangers that all computer users must be aware of:

1. **An increase in hijacked and spoofed e-mail addresses.** Spammers have discovered new ways to make it appear as though their spam e-mail is coming from your computer. This could result in having your Internet connection terminated or put on hold by your internet provider - all without your knowledge.
2. **An increase in virus-carrying spam.** Accidentally open a spam e-mail carrying a nasty virus and you can end up with big problems ranging from the slowing of your system to more serious threats such as system crashes, data loss, identity theft, redirecting your web browser to porn sites, and more.
3. **Phishing spam.** A phishing e-mail appears to be a legitimate e-mail from a bank, vendor, friend, or other trusted source. The purpose is to trick you into giving confidential information such as bank accounts, social security numbers, passwords, and credit card information. You've probably already received a PayPal or bank spam e-mail that said your account was going to be closed unless you verified your information. It then directs you to a very convincing web site where you input certain information the spammer is trying to glean. In reality, this is a malicious third party that is going to use your information to open credit card accounts, access your account, steal money, and cause you other major identity and financial problems.

Pragmatic Solution

First and foremost, it's absolutely critical that you get a quality spam blocking software installed as a first line of defense. New government regulations haven't done a single thing towards preventing or stopping spammers so the responsibility lies on your shoulders.

Next, you want to make sure you don't throw yourself under the bus by getting on a spammers list in the first place. Once you're on a spammer's list, it's impossible to get off and changing your e-mail address can be a major inconvenience especially if you rely on it to stay in touch with important business and personal contacts.

To reduce the chances of your e-mail address getting on a spammer's list, here are 5 simple preventative measures you can take that will go a long way in keeping not-so-delicious spam out of your in-box.

1. **Use a disposable e-mail address.**

   If you buy products online or occasionally subscribe to web sites that interest you, chances are you're going to get spammed.

   To avoid your main e-mail address from ending up on their broadcast list, set up a free Internet e-mail address with Yahoo or Google and use it when buying or opting in to online newsletters. You can also use a throwaway e-mail address when making purchases or subscribing to newsletters (see #4 below). It will keep your main email accounts from getting clogged up.

2. **Pay attention to check boxes that automatically opt you in.**

   Whenever you subscribe to a web site or make a purchase online be very watchful of small, pre-checked boxes that say, "Yes! I want to receive offers from third party companies."

If you do not un-check the box to opt-out, your e-mail address can (and will) be sold to every online advertiser. To avoid this from happening simply take a closer look at every online form you fill out.

3. **Don't post your main e-mail address on your web site, web forums, or newsgroups.**

Spammers have special programs that can glean e-mail addresses from web sites without your permission. If you are posting to a web forum or newsgroup, use your disposable e-mail address instead of your main e-mail address.

If you want to post an e-mail address on your home page, use "info@" and have all replies forwarded to a folder in your in-box that won't interfere with your main address. Better yet would be to use a contact form.

4. **Create throwaway e-mail accounts.**

If you own a web domain, all mail going to an address at your domain is probably set up to come directly to you by default. For example, an e-mail addressed to anything@yourdomain.com will be delivered to your in-box.

This is a great way to fight spam without missing out on important e-mails you want to get. The next time you sign up for a newsletter use the title of the web site in your e-mail address. For example, if the web site is entitled "www.greatwidgets.com," enter "greatwidgets@yourdomain.com" as your e-mail address. If you get spammed, look at what address the spam was sent to.

If greatwidgets@yourdomain.com shows up as the original recipient, you know the source since that e-mail address was unique to that web site. Now you can easily stop the spam by making any e-mail sent to that address bounce back to the sender.

> **5. Don't open, reply to, or try to opt-out of obvious spam e-mails.**
>
> Opening, replying to, or even clicking a bogus opt-out link in an obvious spam e-mail signals that your e-mail address is active and more spam will follow.
>
> The only time it is safe to click on the opt-out link or reply to the e-mail is when the message was sent from a company you know or do business with (for example, a company that you purchase from or a newsletter you subscribed to).

It is also important to understand what is leaving your network. An infected computer may become a member of a bot-net. A bot-net is a network of compromised computers that collectively receive their orders from a central authority and can be used to set up distributed attacks, steal confidential information, or more likely distribute more spam. Spam that is being sent from your network (whether it comes from your email systems or not) will not only slow down your network but it will get your email system blacklisted and your legitimate email marked as spam.

Since all software is written by humans and humans make mistakes, software constantly needs to be kept up to date. Running some antivirus on your computer will not prevent all attacks, it is just a layer of defense (and, if it doesn't have the latest database, a useless layer at that!). Unfortunately, this isn't always an easy proposition. Although some software vendors, like Microsoft, provide a scheduled release of patches to their operating systems and applications, most others don't. Sometimes these mistakes in software code or bugs can be exploited by malicious software writers in order to gain access to your system. It is a "back-door" of sorts that will allow the attacker to drop in a small program that allows them further access to either have your computer join a bot-net as discussed, download more malicious code, or steal information.

> **Pragmatic Solution**
>
> Some software applications will provide an automated check to see if it's running the latest releases and patches of their programs. At the very least, these should be used. Although this doesn't provide assurances that every patch is in place, it is essentially better than nothing. Your IT manager should have the tools and capability in place to assure that the patches are being applied and applied successfully. The first step is knowing what applications you are running and then put together a regular program that checks to ensure you are running the latest versions of these applications.

Probably the most important thing you can do as a business owner to ensure that you reduce the exposure and threats to your information is to lead by example. If keeping your information safe is important to you, and you ingrain that in your corporate culture so your employees also are aware of the risks and the consequences of those risks around them, you're done right? Well, if you then turn around and break your own rules, it does not send a proper signal to your employees. They will see that the rules are just theater and will work around them rather than with them.

Not limited to risk awareness, when employees see that their managers takes issues seriously enough that they follow it themselves, the employee will work doubly hard to do the same. If employers not only expect that level of commitment, stick to it themselves, and reward those that go above and beyond, you've done better than 80% of companies out there.

Chapter 6

Tips in Renting or Buying Commercial Real Estate

By Helene Strumeyer

Whether you're just starting out a new business in a retail space or your home based business is ready for the next big step (commercial office space), the following 10 tips will be critical in getting you prepared in your next big step of leasing commercial real estate.

1. Leave yourself enough time: <u>Expect the process from start to finish to take anywhere from six months to a year.</u> Start looking for your space one year in advance. Plan accordingly. However, that being said, in depressed areas or tough economic times you might just find a great deal which could close much faster.

2. <u>Be aware of the up-front expense</u>. If you have ever rented an apartment or a house, you are used to the concept of one and a half month's rent (at maximum by law in most states) for security deposit. You may encounter two things completely different in leasing commercial real estate. The first is that the leasing company or owner may require six to eight months of security up front (or more). This much adds up to a very large sum. ($3,000 a month x 8 months equals a total of $24,000!) Secondly, they may require hard

real estate as collateral such as your personal home but only if it has equity covering a specified amount.

3. <u>Hire a Commercial Real Estate Broker</u>: Typically, HIRING A COMMERCIAL BROKER DOES NOT COST YOU - THE TENANT/BUYER. In most instances when buying or leasing a commercial space the LANDLORD pays the broker's commission. This is vastly different when in many areas of the country people are accustomed to being the one to pay any realtor fee as a residential renter. It is best to check in your area with an experienced agent as this practice can be a regionalized custom.

4. <u>A broker can help you avoid hidden costs</u>. For example, you think you are getting a great deal on an office space, full gross, all included. Here's just one example of something that can cost you more money. Often, Tenants pay a portion of the increase in taxes and other items, calculated by base year. So say a Tenant's base year is 2010 and they move in 2014. In 2015, they will pay a portion of the increase from 2010. If the broker had insisted on a base year of 2014, in 2015, when they had to start paying their portion of the tax increase, the calculation is based on one year not five. (As 2014 would be the starting calculation date instead of 2010.)

5. <u>Hiring a commercial Broker that specializes in your type of product (i.e. office or warehouse vs. retail specialist) instead of a "generalist"</u>. Rental rates often are more consistent between areas vs. towns.

6. <u>Never Hire a residential broker to find you commercial space</u>. Trust me it makes a difference. If you put a gun to my head, I wouldn't know how to sell a house as I am highly specialized in commercial real estate. The same is true even more so in reverse. Purchasing or leasing space is

often the largest investment a business makes. Find someone who knows what they are doing. As with anything, ask other business owners for referrals.

7. <u>Be open to location</u>. Rates can vary widely from town to town even in the case of neighboring towns or cities.

8. <u>The build out of the space office or warehouse may be a cost to your business.</u> Tenant Improvement is not always included in the price but it could be to a negotiated extent. This is a detail that when negotiated properly can save you thousands and make the right real estate agent worth their weight in gold.

9. <u>Ask your Broker whether the state or city offers tax credits for moving from another country, state, or city.</u> For example, New Jersey offers substantial tax credits and/or incentives for moving.

10. <u>Find a broker who is a Problem Solver, not a Salesperson</u>. There are always issues during the last 5% of the deal that can make or break a deal. An experienced and talented broker will navigate the issues and resolve them. Once again, be sure to ask another business owner for a referral.

Chapter 7

Life and Health Insurance for the Business Owner

By Harry Herbst

Being a small business owner today, especially in this economy, is no easy proposition. Salaries aside, employee benefits are the single largest expense for any business owner. In an economy where small business profits can be down (in many cases) by fifty-percent, the cost of benefits on average still increase in the neighborhood of twenty-five percent each year. This, along with increased expenses across the board in other areas, is enough to give any small business owner significant anxiety. Of course, in this day and age, employees are being asked to contribute a larger percentage into the employee benefit pool and, if the math doesn't work out for the small business owner, then hours get reduced and employees start to lose their jobs.

When we speak of benefits we are speaking for the most part about health insurance so we will focus our discussion on this. A decade ago most business owners had a one-hundred percent plan that included out-of-network benefits. Year after year these benefits are significantly "watered down". Fast forward to today and it is not difficult to see that the benefits that employees receive are but a fraction of what they were in another time and place.

First:

> A separate deductible for those who have been hospitalized known as a hospital co-pay rider.

Second:

> A split co-payment in the form of a higher co-payment for specialists versus your primary care physician. For example, a visit to your primary care physician may cost $20 whereas a trip to the specialist is $50. A primary care physician today is inclusive of an internist, obstetrician, or pediatrician. All others are more or less considered to be specialists.

The elimination of out-of-network coverage is basically known as a Health Maintenance Organization (HMO). What this means is that in order to be covered you must use all in-network services. If the physician does not participate in your plan, then you do not have reimbursable benefits. Most small businesses utilize an HMO type of plan.

A one-hundred percent plan is indicative of no out-of-pocket expenses. Today's plans more closely resemble eighty, seventy, or even fifty percent plans that are indicative of having to satisfy a deductible before coverage begins.

<u>Out of pocket expenses</u>: Prescription drug benefits. As medications become more expensive, this requires the participant to have greater out of pocket expenses. Rx benefits are one of the major contributors to increases in insurance premiums. The elimination of some basic services such as MRI's, cat scans, and other services become out of pocket expenses in an effort to reduce premiums. Concurrently, premiums continue to sky rocket.

Ancillary benefits such as dental and vision benefits have become luxury benefits and unaffordable to many small business owners whereas a decade ago it was considered mainstream for these benefits to be covered.

Chapter 8

Goal Setting: Obtain Your Business Objectives

By Arnie Rentzler, Certified Business Coach

Defining your purpose, establishing your values, and developing success-oriented attitudes will give your life meaning and will give you a sense of direction. It will not, however, ensure success. Only goal setting, planning, and working your plan will do that. Your vision of the future you would like, if turned into goals and taken through the proper planning process, can dramatically affect the quality and fullness of your life. Goal setting is a powerful tool for higher levels of achievement. However, goals are only as attainable as your belief in your ability to attain them.

Lofty goals set by someone with a lack of confidence are as realistic as building a skyscraper on quicksand. They will get swallowed up and lost in the muck and mire of daily survival. A vision of a future filled with happiness, achievement, and success, created by a person with a low self-image, is destined to remain an elusive dream. However, a clear vision of a successful future, fueled by passion and developed by a person with a positive self-image, is destined to become reality.

Goal setting and planning will help you manage your life as well as your time. Focusing on your goals and on the rewards must become a habit. To develop this habit, begin and end each day with a review (and a reminder) of your goals and what's important to you. Note your progress. Evaluate your priorities and carefully choose your upcoming activities.

Whether your objectives are great or small, you can achieve more of them more often by addressing these questions:

1. What do I want to do?

2. How can I accomplish this goal?

3. What steps need to be taken to get started?

4. What obstacles are in my way?

5. How do I overcome them?

Establish goals and priorities in both your business and personal life. Organize your time to ensure realization of goals in both areas. You will find forms for crystallizing both your personal and business goals in the appropriate sections. Getting organized and feeling in control will contribute significantly to a life filled with achievement and satisfaction. Establishing and working toward goals that are important to you will add excitement and meaning to everything you do.

You might want to ask yourself these questions:

- Does work become a source of fulfillment - a place and activity where many of your personal needs can be satisfied?
- Do you feel like your day is providing value?
- Do you recognize the importance of your personal life?
- Do you give your family, friends, and hobbies priority?
- Do you enjoy your leisure time?
- Do you plan time for personal improvement and relaxation?
- Do your personal goals include goals in all six major life areas: Mental, Social, Physical, Financial, Family, and Spiritual?
- Do they include short and long-range tangible and intangible goals?

Your goals, both personnel and professional, should include "becoming" goals as well as "having" or "attaining" goals. One will affect the other. For example, if you want to "have" more money, chances are that you must "become" worth more. You may have to become better at your job, better at another job, or perhaps even in another capacity. If you want to "have" more time to spend with your family, you have to "become" more organized at work. If you want to "have" greater respect and loyalty from others, you may have to "become" more deserving of respect and loyalty. To have, you must become. It is always useful to remember that, in life, investment always comes before reward.

Many people go through life without ever identifying what they want, where they want to go, or who they want to become. They get so caught up in day-to-day living that they fail to decide what they want to accomplish. They wonder why they feel frustrated, never achieving anything significant. It would be in their interest to realize the difficulty of hitting something they've never visualized or returning from somewhere they've never been. People who have no goals have no direction. They go around in circles, always moving, but never arriving or achieving.

Look at yourself honestly and squarely. Ask yourself: "What do I want to do and who do I want to be?" Crystallize your dreams and goals. List all those things that you'd like to have, to achieve, to see, or to be. Continue to add to your list and review it frequently, noting those goals that you achieve

When setting your goals, be specific. Make sure that you can measure achievement. Goals such as "increased sales," or "lower costs," are not nearly as powerful as goals such as "Create 10 new clients," or "lower costs by $100,000.00," Your goals should be realistically high providing a need to stretch to achieve them. The often heard quote: "Man's reach should exceed his grasp, else what's heaven for?" sums up much of the motivational power of goals that are high enough to excite us.

Crystallize your goals. Writing them down helps you to focus and enhances commitment. If you share them with others, you can increase your commitment. Goals should always have target dates. This helps to build urgency and to prioritize your day-to-day activities and projects. And finally, remember to balance your goals between your personal and professional pursuits. Plan time for both. Too much work or too much play can wreak havoc in life. Without balance, even the sure-footed stumble and fall. Consider the mighty Roman Empire. The ancient Romans climbed to greatness, conquering neighboring lands and people. But once a vast empire was built, stretching from Britain to the Orient, the hard work and perseverance began to wane. The scales tipped to too much celebration and merriment. Under Nero, Rome celebrated 176 legal holidays each year. Imagine…almost every other day was a day of leisure! And we all know what eventually happened to the Roman Empire.

To be successful does NOT require stress, overexertion, a meaningless personal life, failed relationships or a mercenary attitude. The person who enjoys his or her work, feels that he is doing something of value, and has other relationships, commitments, and activities outside of work that are seen as being of value, is a success. The healthy person has both a successful career aand a rewarding personal life. This does not mean that, from time-to-time, one or the other may ttake a back seat for a short time. For example, the salesperson starting a new territory may have to put in 80-100 hour weeks for about six months. A new parent may choose to spend time at home bonding and caring for a new child. Later that same year, a parent may focus on work so that he or she can provide for that same child's education.

When setting your goals, addressing balance is key. Be sure that you have goals in your personal as well as professional life. Just as all sun and no rain make a desert, all work and no play make a dull life.

STAYING S.M.A.R.T.

One way to test your goals is to run them through the SMART test. Goals should be **Specific, Measurable, Achievable, Realistically high, and Target dates should be established**. Once you have established goals and determined priorities, the daily decisions become much easier because you have set parameters. Being goal-directed is not an intellectual exercise…it's a way of life. Every meeting, every telephone call, every transaction is focused. You are constantly asking yourself: What's my goal…for this meeting…for this interview…for this day?

In the absence of clearly defined goals, everything becomes a crisis, everyone becomes a task-master, and everything becomes urgent. You fall into the trap of becoming reactive rather than proactive. In the react mode, you will feel pressured, stressed, out of control, and filled with anxiety. When you are proactive, you will feel in control and powerful. Feelings of satisfaction and achievement spur you on to even greater accomplishment. Anytime you find yourself in the react mode evaluate your goals, focus on your vision, organize your work, plan your activities, and work your plan.

STRESS MANAGEMENT

If you continue to accept more than you can handle, you end up with many balls in the air, lots of responsibility, and lots of things to do. You also end up feeling overworked, underpaid, and unfulfilled. These feelings conflict with the basic human need to be appreciated, to be recognized and rewarded, and to live a fulfilling life. By taking on too much (in the quest for self-importance) many people end up feeling pressured and then make mistakes. If you promise too much to too many and find yourself unable to keep your promises, you feel guilty. All too often because you feel guilty you promise even more and feel even more guilt. The process diminishes your self-worth and causes others to be frustrated and a vicious circle continues and grows. How do you stop? Decide to not dance anymore to someone else's tune! Refuse to accept more than you can handle or anything that's not compatible with your purpose and your goals. Redesign how your work is performed.

Ask yourself: "What am I trying to prove? Who am I trying to please? How much of what I am doing is because I choose and how much is because I feel compelled to please others or to prove my worth?" Many people who take on too much are trying to show others that they are worthy. In their excessive need to please others, they deprive themselves.

Don't set yourself up to fail or create imbalance by taking on too much or too much in one area at the expense of another. If you do, you will create stress. Stress is frequently self-imposed because we fail to plan, we schedule ourselves to be in two or three places at one time, or we agree to complete projects in days that should take weeks.

What are the top five sources of stress in your life?

1.

2.

3.

4.

5.

Which of these can you change by planning your activities differently?

1.

2.

3.

For those that can't be changed can you reframe the situation for a different outcome? For example, look upon your dealings with a demanding boss as proof that you can handle any difficult situation or person. If you can learn to view stressful situations as opportunities for growth, you will relieve stress by taking control and developing a new attitude. If you can't control the situation, your best bet is to control the way you regard the situation.

When someone comes to you with a problem that you don't have time to solve or one that actually could be better solved by someone else, return it to them immediately. A suggestion like "I'd like you to think about this situation and come up with several possible solutions and then we'll discuss the solutions" or "I will not have time to address this until I finish the current projects I am working on. Could someone else help you faster?"

If you have allowed yourself to get over-committed, you've got some choices:

1. Continue doing the same things you've been doing.

2. Work more hours.

3. Lower your goals and/or standards.

4. Delegate.

5. Improve your time management skills and work habits.

6. Make decisions based on your purpose and your goals.

Consider what is important and .what you want to achieve in your life. Challenge anything that is not compatible with your goals and/or priorities.

OVERCOMING PROCRASTINATION

In any endeavor, there are barriers everyone faces at one time or another. Perhaps the most common one is a stalling tactic that you may call upon either consciously or subconsciously (i.e. procrastination). You may remember it from your high school or college days when students thought it was "cool" to "cram" the night before the big exam. You may recognize it in a spouse or relative who talks about Christmas shopping for months and then lets it all go until December 24th. You may even take comfort in the fact that procrastination is a habit of the masses. One look at the post office lines on April 15th is enough to confirm that fact as everyone tries to file tax returns before the stroke of midnight.

Procrastination is the habit of needlessly putting off things that we should do or say we should do, now. Procrastination can be caused by negative attitudes or fear of failure. It can be rooted in our own inertia or as a result of lack of planning. It does more than almost any other habit we have to deprive us of satisfaction, success, and happiness. More than two centuries ago, Edward Young wrote: "Procrastination is the thief of time."

In fact, procrastination is much more. It is the thief of our self-respect. It deprives us of the fullest realization of our ambitions and hopes. In business, it can even cause or contribute heavily to our failure. "He who hesitates is truly lost."

When things are put off until the last minute, we create pressure. Every step finds an impediment. We push ourselves into blundering by having to make hasty decisions and judgments and it actually becomes harder to do things. Haste does make waste.

Herein lies the paradox. By trying to make things easy we do not make them easy. We actually make things harder. The first step in overcoming the tendency to procrastinate is to understand why you behave the way you do and what kinds of situations cause you to take action.

None of us needs to look beyond himself or herself for examples of how procrastination has thwarted our goals of achievement. Do you remember postponing that report that you should have done Wednesday? On Thursday and Friday you found yourself loaded with important jobs and had to work over the weekend (to get it ready for that Monday morning meeting) or perhaps you postponed visiting a sick relative only to hear that it was too late? Many salespeople have lost an account to a competitor because they put off deciding how to approach a difficult prospect.

No one escapes his or her quota of difficult or unpleasant tasks. It is often these unpleasant tasks that contribute most to our success. You will learn a great lesson when you realize that they will not fade away if you ignore them or procrastinate. Eventually, it's best to roll up your sleeves and wade into them. We work more effectively when we create a habit of doing the unpleasant things first and getting them out of the way so that we can do the things that we like to do later.

Do not allow an obstacle or difficulty to become an excuse. Instead of "I'm tired, I'll do it tomorrow," try "I'm tired and I'll just work for another half hour and then go to bed." Reward yourself **after** you've completed something. Instead of thinking "I'll never get this done" allow yourself the coffee break or other time out that you want after completing one part of the assignment. Remember, the journey of a thousand miles begins with a single step.

You do not see listless people at the top of the success ladder. As Samuel Smiles said: "People who are habitually behind in their work are as habitually behind in success."

As a general rule, it is wise to make decisions promptly and crisply rather than lingering over them. In a competitive world, timing is critical. By waiting for precisely the right time, you may be much too late.

The well-organized life and business leave time for everything – for planning, doing, and following through. To the procrastinator, time is like a taskmaster with a whip. To the organized, action-oriented person that same amount of time is like a savings account where the interest keeps growing. You have the power and ability to manage your time or to have it manage you.

If you are not where you want to be or who you want to be, make different choices. You have the power to choose where you live, with whom you live, and how you live. You have the power to choose where you work, what you do, and the quality of your work. You choose your level of success or failure based on how you choose to spend or invest your time.

Is your desk covered with tons work to be done, projects to review, and letters that require a response? Does your "To Do" list seem to grow longer and longer regardless of your efforts? Do you ever feel overworked, underpaid, and unappreciated?

Or, is your energy level at an all-time high? Do you always finish your work before you leave and find yourself able to give each project or person ample attention? Finally, are you spending enough quality time enjoying your family, friends, and personal hobbies?

If you have ever had a day in which you felt as if you worked hard with long hours and still got nothing accomplished, you need to get organized. If important matters are regularly pushed aside so that you can put out a fire or address a crisis, you need to get organized. Does a life filled with personal and professional achievements with plenty of time to relax and enjoy the fruits of your labor – and above all, living *your* values and *your* goals – describe *your* life? Or does this seem like an unattainable dream? If you, like many of other people, have let your life get out of control...relax. Regaining control and living a life that provides you with tangible and intangible rewards is more achievable than you think.

In the rapidly changing, very time-conscious world in which we live, effective time management is important because it provides a necessary focus to help to get more done...with fewer people...in less time.

There used to be a great number of companies and time specialists that promoted and sold "unique" calendar planning systems as the answer to all of one's organizational challenges. Now we have gone to computers, smart phones, and tablets for the most part. Yet you can still open almost any magazine that focuses on improvement and you'll find an article about time management. There are almost as many time-management "secrets" as there are weight-loss "secrets." Each promises you a magic formula to help you realize success with little or no effort. The fact is that success without effort is an anomaly and there is no "secret" to effective time management. There are several techniques that can work and it really doesn't matter if you use Google Calendar, Outlook, or a traditional paper based system. **What matters is not what system you use, but that you use a system.** What matters is that you prioritize your activities and actions and set meaningful goals. And what really matters is that the system you use works for you so YOU can achieve more in less time and have more discretionary time to enjoy the fruits of your labors.

Time management is a skill, a technique, a mindset, and a lifestyle. It can be learned by anyone who:

- has a desire to get more out of his or her life
- wants to feel more in control
- wants to achieve success in business while enjoying the pleasures of a personal life
- Wants to reduce stress and realize more balance in life

While achieving effective time-management is not easy and no habit change is, time management is a matter of replacing less-than-effective habits with better ones. It is fairly simple. In fact, you probably already have a head start!

The truth is that almost everyone has a fairly good understanding of the basic time management techniques. Almost everyone knows how to plan and prioritize. Most know they should be more organized. The problem is that very few of us always do that which we know we should do.

It is important that we have a successful time management system. Think in your mind about someone you believe is very successful. Does that person keep his or her word? The answer is probably yes. If we keep our word consistently, we create power in our lives. The more powerful we are (i.e. the ability to have things and events be the way we want them to be) the more effective we are. The more effective we are the better we feel. What is the first thing we need to do before we keep our word? It is to give our word. That creates the POTENTIAL for us to keep our word which in turn creates POWER for us to be effective and feel good and, therefore, to be more effective. We call this "THE FORMULA FOR WELL BEING".

```
                         P                    P
                         O                    O    Feel Good
    Give Your Word       T    Keep Your Word  W    --------
                         E                    E    Effective
                         N                    R
                         T
                         I
                         A
                         L
```

EVALUATING CURRENT BEHAVIOR AND HABITS

While there are ideas and techniques that have stood the test of time and will help you get more out of your time, one's primary focus should not be on external systems, "skills", and "knowledge." Rather one should focus on attitudes, internal feelings, and habits. Focus on learning how to harness the natural energy that comes when you are doing something that is exciting and meaningful to you. Focus on developing the mental confidence, empowering attitudes, and a life-planning process that will give you back control of your life and help you to live it in a fuller, richer, and more satisfying way. Achieving more, feeling better, and becoming more successful has more to do with your internal attitudes, self-esteem, goals, and aspirations than with external events.

If you attempt to change behavior through utilizing a new time management system, prioritizing in a different way, or any of the other available techniques without addressing the way you think and feel or who and what you value and what your goals are, any success will be limited and short-lived at best.

CREATING A STRONG FOUNDATION

Your behavior is influenced by your mental and emotional outlook which is part of your attitude. That's why developing healthy fulfilling attitudes is such a critical part of time management. Your ability to manage your time will be governed in large measure by your ability to manage your life. It will also be influenced by your goals and how important they are to you. **In the end, time management is not a time management issue; it is a personal and professional goals clarification issue.**

In any change process we must examine the three keys to achieving higher levels of success and getting more enjoyment out of that success:

#1: **Attitudes.** The foundation for success in any area is developing a success-oriented attitude about yourself and others. While this may sound like a trite cliché, the fact of the matter is that what you do is influenced by how you think, and how you think is founded in your most basic attitudes.

 # 2: Skills. Identifying, developing, and continuously improving the skills, both technical and non-technical, which we will utilize to achieve our goals is a critical link in the achievement chain.

#3: Goals. Both professionally and personally, goals provide direction and purpose to living a life filled with achievement, prosperity, and happiness. A successful life is a balanced life. Success is the continuous achievement of your own predetermined goals stabilized by balance and purified by belief in both your personal and professional life.

All too often, we live our lives as if we had an unending supply of days. Unfortunately, that is simply not the case. We are only here for a visit. Each of us has a certain number of days on this earth. While that number varies, one truism does not vary: some people get much more out of just a few days while others seem to spend a lifetime accomplishing nothing. There are twenty-four hours in a day for everyone. Yet some seem to accomplish much while many take an inordinate amount of time to do little. For each of us, both of these phenomena periodically occur. On certain days, we accomplish a great deal and time just seems to fly by. All of a sudden we look at our watches and are surprised by the lateness of the hour. On other days, everything seems to be in slow motion. Minutes seem like hours and hours seem like days.

The quantity of time doesn't really change. There are always sixty seconds in a minute, sixty minutes in an hour, and twenty-four hours in a day. What changes is not time. What changes is our perception and perception is our reality. When we are having fun working at challenging and stimulating projects directly related to our goals, our achievement level skyrockets and time flies. When we are bored or doing something we don't like, we're constantly checking the time which drags as does our level of accomplishment. When we feel "under the gun", "behind the eight ball", and "out of control" time seems to go too fast. We feel out of control and stressed, unable to get done what we need to accomplish in the time allotted, and are forever behind on our projects. Since we cannot increase or manufacture more time, we must get more out of the time we have.

If we return to our original premise that almost all of us know how to manage our time and that we realize the value of becoming more effective at managing our time, why don't more of us do a better job of doing so? We all know what we *should* do. NIKE made famous the "Just do it!" slogan. For most of us, that's easy to say but difficult to do. Why? To answer that question, we must first look at the factors that influence our behavior.

ATTITUDES

Our behavior is influenced by our desires and our thoughts. The way we think is influenced by our attitudes. Our attitudes are developed through a conditioning process that began very early in life. These attitudes continue to be a dominant force in determining our success or failure in all areas including our ability to manage our time and control our lives. By examining the future and the past, you will develop a much better understanding of why you do the things you do. This insight will help you to improve your ability to manage your time and your life and to ensure that a full and rewarding future is your destiny.

We must begin by examining our early conditioning and existing attitudes. Before you begin to think about changing your attitudes, you must first examine the ones that you've already developed.

Take the time to crystallize your vision and your values and, as a result, evaluate the effectiveness of your current attitudes. It is helpful to understand more about your existing attitudes and how and why you make some of the decisions that you make. It is also helpful to examine the effect early conditioning has on behavior and attitudes. If early conditioning was predominately nurturing and encouraging, a person is likely to mature into an adult who views trying new things with positive anticipation and has only a small degree of fear of failure. As a child, were you encouraged to try new things? Were your efforts recognized with positive accolades? Or were your attempts forgotten and your failures rewarded with admonitions and warnings? If your early environment and conditioning was supportive and encouraging, you probably find it relatively easy to accept new challenges. However, if your early conditioning was very judgmental and you typically received harsh criticism for mistakes, you will probably tend to stay with the "safe" and "known" tasks where you know what to do.

If a person was raised in what many view as a "traditional" environment where early admonitions were the norm and "good manners" the benchmark, that person may avoid new challenges for fear of criticism or reprisal. Did you hear things like "Speak your mind regardless of who disagrees with you?" or (and more likely) did you hear, "Children should be seen and not heard!" or "Don't talk to strangers!" or "Don't go where you're not wanted!" and other negative admonitions? As a result, do you sometimes find yourself uncomfortable in new situations or hesitant to suggest a new idea?

If much of our early rewards as children came from doing everything we were told to do and that was what we learned, which made us feel successful and now we find that we cannot possibly do everything on our plate all of the time perfectly, is it any wonder that maybe we feel overwhelmed and NOT successful or in control.

DEVELOPING TIME-CONSCIOUS ATTITUDES

The first step in changing *any* habit is to identify the habit that you want to change. This is true for your habits about time attitudes as well. Establish a period of time to analyze your attitudes, behavior, situations, and outcomes. Evaluate your present use of time. Recording exactly how you spend your time is an important discovery process. Most people have a very inaccurate understanding of just how they actually spend their time.

Create an accurate time analysis that will help you to pinpoint who and what occupies your time. To ensure accuracy, do not try to rely on your memory and attempt to "complete" your analysis at the end of the day. Keep it with you and note everything you do as you do it. Before you can control your time and develop better time management habits, you must understand or identify existing habits

After you consolidate your data and evaluate your time use, look for activities that you may want to delegate or eliminate; look for time wasters and peak performance periods. Pinpoint precise behaviors that are incompatible with your vision, goals, and values. For example, if your goals include getting a promotion which will mean an increase in salary but yet you keep making commitments to your friends and family that will keep you from excelling at work, your behavior is inconsistent with your goals. If your early approval was dependent upon doing for others and you find yourself regularly taking on more than you can handle, your behavior is understandable although self-defeating.

Examine your attitudes and determine if a change in thinking is warranted. If your goal is to make more sales but you avoid sales-oriented activities, your behavior is inconsistent with your goals. If you want to achieve outstanding success but you work minimal hours and exert only average effort, your behavior is inconsistent with your goals. You can either change your goals to be more inspiring and motivating so as to propel you to do more or you can change your behavior by developing new habits of thinking and habits of doing.

It is important to define the new habit that you wish to develop. Be as specific as possible. For example, if you wish to develop a more balanced life and feel more in control, you might take a personal-development course that will help you to develop your skills in setting and achieving goals. If you want to develop habits conducive to success in business, you might read autobiographies of those successful in business or participate in a personal development process.

Just as negative habits in our lives can be undermining and destructive, positive ones can be uplifting and forwarding of our goals. Building habits requires defining very precise behaviors and performing them at specific times, motivated by deeply held values. As Aristotle said, "We are what we repeatedly do." We can identify what we want to become and become it.

Be meticulous about your daily planning process. Plan tomorrow before you finish today. Both self-discipline and self-management are critical aspects of time management and both of these can be developed. Focus on your rewards.

Crystallize your rewards to yourself and make a note of them so that you are reminded of them often. Your rewards must exceed in value the price you'll pay in effort or you will be inclined to revert to old habits. Once you decide to do something, make a promise to yourself to continue until you win! Keep your promises! Take responsibility for your own success or failure. Recognize the value of a long-term benefit rather than momentary gratification.

Develop a winner's attitude. Think positively about your opportunities, your potential, your ability to achieve your goals, and your right to success. Focus your thoughts. Train yourself to seek solutions and not to place blame and to focus on that which you can control and not on that which you can't. If you break an iron rod at its weakest point and weld it back together again, the weakest point becomes the strongest point. Your weaknesses, if faced head on, can become your greatest strengths. Don't run away from things just because you're frightened. If you do, you'll always be afraid.

Chapter 9

Time Management: We All Get The Same 24 Hours in a Day – Learn the Secrets to Making the Most of Your Time

By Arnie Rentzler, Certified Business Coach

Is your desk covered with tons work to be done, projects to review, and letters that require a response? Does your "To Do" list seem to grow longer and longer regardless of your efforts? Do you ever feel overworked, underpaid, and unappreciated?

Or, is your energy level at an all-time high? Do you always finish your work before you leave, and find yourself able to give each project or person ample attention? And finally, are you spending enough quality time enjoying your family, friends, and personal hobbies?

If you have ever had a day in which you felt as if you worked hard with long hours and still got nothing accomplished, you need to get organized. If important matters are regularly pushed aside so that you can put out a fire, or address a crisis, you need to get organized. Does a life filled with personal and professional achievements, with plenty of time to relax and enjoy the fruits of your labor – and above all, living *your* values and *your* goals – describe *your* life? Or does this seem like an unattainable dream? If you, like many of other people, have let your life get out of control…relax. Regaining control and living a life that provides you with tangible and intangible rewards is more achievable than you think.

In the rapidly changing, very time-conscious world in which we live, effective time management is important because it provides a necessary focus to help to get more done…with fewer people…in less time.

There used to be a great number of companies and time specialists that promoted and sold "unique" calendar planning systems as the answer to all of one's organizational challenges. Now we have gone to computers, smart phones and tablets, for the most part. Yet, you can still open almost any magazine that focuses on improvement and you'll find an article about time management. There are almost as many time-management "secrets" as there are weight-loss "secrets." Each promises you a magic formula to help you realize success with little or no effort. The fact is that success without effort is an anomaly, and there is no "secret" to effective time management. There are several techniques that can work, and it really doesn't matter if you use Google Calendar, Outlook or a traditional paper based system. **What matters is not what system you use, but that you use a system.** What matters is that you prioritize your activities and actions and set meaningful goals. And what really matters is that the system you use works for you…so YOU can achieve more in less time and have more discretionary time to enjoy the fruits of your labors.

Time management is a skill, a technique, a mindset, and a lifestyle. It can be learned by anyone who:

- has a desire to get more out of his or her life,
- wants to feel more in control,
- wants to achieve success in business while enjoying the pleasures of a personal life
- Wants to reduce stress and realize more balance in life.

While achieving effective time-management is not easy, and no habit change is time management is a matter of replacing less- than-effective habits with better ones. It is fairly simple. In fact, you probably already have a head start!

The truth is that almost everyone has a fairly good understanding of the basic time management techniques. Almost everyone knows how to plan and prioritize. Most know they should be more organized. The problem is that very few of us always do that which we know we should do.

It is important that we have a successful Time Management System. Think in your mind about someone you believe is very successful. Does that person keep his or her word? The answer is probably yes. If we keep our word consistently, we create power in our lives. The more powerful we are - i.e. the ability to have things and events be the way we want them to be - the more effective we are. The more effective we are, the better we feel. What is the first thing we need to do before we keep our word? It is to give our word. That creates the POTENTIAL for us to keep our word, which in turn creates POWER for us to be effective and feel good, and therefore to be more effective. We call this 'THE FORMULA FOR WELL BEING'.

```
                        P              P
                        O              O    Feel Good
    Give Your Word    T Keep Your Word   W   --------
                        E              E    Effective
                        N              R
                        T
                        I
                        A
                        L
```

EVALUATING CURRENT BEHAVIOR AND HABITS

While there are ideas and techniques that have stood the test of time and will help you get more out of your time, one's primary focus should not be on external systems, "skills" and "knowledge." Rather one should focus on attitudes, internal feelings, and habits. Focus on learning how to harness the natural energy that comes when you are doing something that is exciting and meaningful to you. Focus on developing the mental confidence, empowering attitudes, and a life-planning process that will give you back control of your life and help you to live it in a fuller, richer, and more satisfying way. Achieving more, feeling better, and becoming more successful has more to do with your internal attitudes, self-esteem, goals, and aspirations than with external events.

If you attempt to change behavior through utilizing a new time management system, prioritizing in a different way, or any of the other available techniques without addressing the way you think and feel, who and what you value, and what your goals are, any success will be limited and short-lived at best.

CREATING A STRONG FOUNDATION

Your behavior is influenced by your mental and emotional outlook, your attitudes. That's why developing healthy fulfilling attitudes is such a critical part of time management. Your ability to manage your time will be governed in large measure by your ability to manage your life. It will also be influenced by your goals, and how important they are to you. **In the end, Time Management is not a time management issue; it is a personal and professional goals clarification issue.**

In any change process we must examine the three keys to achieving higher levels of success and getting more enjoyment out of that success:

> #1 Attitudes –The foundation for success in any area is developing a success oriented attitude—about yourself and others. While this may sound like a trite cliché, the fact of the matter is that what you do is influenced by how you think, and how you think is founded in your most basic attitudes.

#2 Skills – Identifying, developing, and continuously improving the skills, both technical and non-technical, which we will utilize to achieve our goals is a critical link in the achievement chain.

#3 Goals – Both professionally and personally, goals provide direction and purpose to living a life filled with achievement, prosperity, and happiness. A successful life is a balanced life. Success is the continuous achievement of your own predetermined goals, stabilized by balance and purified by belief, in both your personal and professional life.

All too often, we live our lives as if we had an unending supply of days. Unfortunately, that is simply not the case. We are only here for a visit. Each of us has a certain number of days on this earth. While that number varies, one truism does not vary: some people get much more out of just a few days, while others seem to spend a lifetime accomplishing nothing. There are twenty-four hours in a day for everyone. Yet, some seem to accomplish much, while many take an inordinate amount of time to do little. For each of us, both of these phenomena periodically occur. On certain days we accomplish a great deal, and time just seems to fly by. All of a sudden we look at our watches and are surprised by the lateness of the hour. On other days, everything seems to be in slow motion. Minutes seem like hours, and hours seem like days.

The quantity of time doesn't really change. There are always sixty seconds in a minute, sixty minutes in an hour, and twenty-four hours in a day. What changes is not time. What changes is our perception, and perception is our reality. When we are having fun working at challenging and stimulating projects directly related to our goals, our achievement level skyrockets and time flies. When we are bored or doing something we don't like, we're constantly checking the time, which drags, as does our level of accomplishment. When we feel "under the gun," "behind the eight ball," and "out of control," time seems to go too fast. We feel out of control and stressed, unable to get done what we need to accomplish in the time allotted, and are forever behind on our projects. Since we cannot increase or manufacture more time, we must get more out of the time we have.

If we return to our original premise that almost all of us know how to manage our time, and that we realize the value of becoming more effective at managing our time, why don't more of us do a better job of doing so? We all know what we _should_ do. NIKE made famous the "Just do it!" slogan. For most of us, that's easy to say, but difficult to do. Why? To answer that question, we must first look at the factors that influence our behavior.

ATTITUDES

Our behavior is influenced by our desires and our thoughts. The way we think is influenced by our attitudes. Our attitudes are developed through a conditioning process that began very early in life. These attitudes continue to be a dominant force in determining our success or failure in all areas, including our ability to manage our time and control our lives. By examining the future and the past, you will develop a much better understanding of why you do the things you do. This insight will help you to improve your ability to manage your time and your life, and to ensure that a full and rewarding future is your destiny.

We must begin by examining our early conditioning and existing attitudes. Before you begin to think about changing your attitudes, you must first examine the ones that you've already developed. Take the time to crystallize your vision and your values and as a result evaluate the effectiveness of your current attitudes It is helpful to understand more about your existing attitudes and how and why you make some of the decisions that you make. It is also helpful to examine the effect early conditioning has on behavior and attitudes. If early conditioning was predominately nurturing and encouraging, a person is likely to mature into an adult who views trying new things with positive anticipation and has only a small degree of fear of failure. As a child, were you encouraged to try new things? Were your efforts recognized with positive accolades? Or were your attempts forgotten and your failures rewarded with admonitions and warnings? If your early environment and conditioning was supportive and encouraging, you probably find it relatively easy to accept new challenges. However, if your early conditioning was very judgmental, and you typically received harsh criticism for mistakes, you will probably tend to stay with the "safe" and "known" tasks where you know what to do.

If a person was raised in what many view as a "traditional" environment where early admonitions were the norm and "good manners" the benchmark, that person may avoid new challenges for fear of criticism or reprisal. Did you hear things like "Speak your mind regardless of who disagrees with you?" or (and more likely) did you hear, "Children should be seen and not heard!" or "Don't talk to strangers!" or "Don't go where you're not wanted!" and other negative admonitions? As a result, do you sometimes find yourself uncomfortable in new situations or hesitant to suggest a new idea?

If much of our early rewards as children came from doing everything we were told to do and that was what we learned that made us feel successful and now we find that we cannot possibly do everything on our plate all of the time perfectly, is it any wonder that maybe we feel overwhelmed and NOT successful or in control.

DEVELOPING TIME-CONSCIOUS ATTITUDES
The first step in changing *any* habit is to identify the habit that you want to change. This is true for your habits about time attitudes as well. Establish a period of time to analyze your attitudes, behavior, situations, and outcomes. Evaluate your present use of time. Recording exactly how you spend your time is an important discovery process. Most people have a very inaccurate understanding of just how they actually spend their time.

Create an accurate time analysis that will help you to pinpoint who and what occupies your time. To ensure accuracy, do not try to rely on your memory and attempt to "complete" your analysis at the end of the day. Keep it with you and note everything you do as you do it. Before you can control your time and develop better time management habits, you must understand or identify existing habits

After you consolidate your data and evaluate your time use, look for activities that you may want to delegate or eliminate; look for time wasters, and peak performance periods. Pinpoint precise behaviors that are incompatible with your vision, goals, and values. For example, if your goals include getting a promotion that will mean an increase in salary, yet you keep making commitments to your friends and family that will keep you from excelling at work, your behavior is inconsistent with your goals. If your early approval was dependent upon doing for others, and you find yourself regularly taking on more than you can handle, your behavior is understandable, although self-defeating.

Examine your attitudes and to determine if a change in thinking is warranted. If your goal is to make more sales but you avoid sales-oriented activities, your behavior is inconsistent with your goals. If you want to achieve outstanding success, but you work minimal hours and exert only average effort, your behavior is inconsistent with your goals. You can either change your goals to be more inspiring and motivating so as to propel you to do more, or you can change your behavior by developing new habits of thinking and habits of doing.

It is important to define the new habit that you wish to develop. Be as specific as possible. For example, if you wish to develop a more balanced life and feel more in control, you might take a personal-development course that will help you to develop your skills in setting and achieving goals. If you want to develop habits conducive to success in business, you might read autobiographies of those successful in business, or participate in a personal development process.

Just as negative habits in our lives can be undermining and destructive, positive ones can be uplifting and forwarding of our goals. Building habits requires defining very precise behaviors and performing them at specific times, motivated by deeply held values. As Aristotle said "We are what we repeatedly do." We can identify what we want to become and become it.

Be meticulous about your daily planning process. Plan tomorrow before you finish today. Both self-discipline and self-management are critical aspects of time management and both of these can be developed. Focus on your rewards.

Crystallize your rewards to yourself and make a note of them so that you are reminded of them often. Your rewards must exceed in value the price you'll pay in effort, or you will be inclined to revert to old habits. Once you decide to do something, make a promise to yourself to continue until you win! Keep your promises! Take responsibility for your own success or failure. Recognize the value of a long-term benefit rather than momentary gratification.

Develop a winner's attitude. Think positively about your opportunities, your potential, your ability to achieve your goals, and your right to success. Focus your thoughts. Train yourself to seek solutions and not to place blame, and to focus on that which you can control, and not on that which you can't. If you break an iron rod at its weakest point and weld it back together again, the weakest point becomes the strongest point. Your weaknesses, if faced head on, can become your greatest strengths. Don't run away from things just because you're frightened. If you do, you'll always be afraid.

Chapter 10

Merchant Services: Understanding the Costs and Uses to Getting New Clients

By Vivian C. Gaspar and Frank Gallipoli

Paying by plastic has become part of our everyday lives. Whether by credit card, debit, EBT, gift cards or simply taking money out of the ATM, society has grown accustomed to carrying any of these. Today even businesses and government agencies issue cards to their employees as a method of payment to simplify accounting. Most banks issue some sort of check or debit card immediately upon opening a checking or savings account.

Sales and cash flow are two of the most important issues that business owners must constantly address. How do I attract more customers to buy my product or use my services? Equally as important, if not more important, is how do I get paid for my services rendered, products sold, or both? In comes Visa, MasterCard, Discover, American Express, etc. to present their services.

The first question that a business owner must ask him or herself is "Will this method of accepting payment be beneficial to the company?" More specifically, will this help increase sales and assist with the cash flow? This question can only be answered if the owner truly understands the company's targeted clients and how those clients prefer to pay. In most cases, the answer is an obvious yes.

If the answer to the first question is yes, then the next question that must be answered is "How do you plan on processing the payments?" This is known as the method of capture. Today cards can be both swiped or manually keyed in. Checks can be scanned and guaranteed without even going to the bank. Customers can even shop and purchase items at 3 am through the merchant's e-commerce site. This will ultimately determine what type of equipment and/or software will be purchased, loaned, or leased to the business. Different merchant service providers have a variety of equipment programs available. It is very important to inquire about these programs and the costs upfront.

You have decided that electronic payments will work for your company and the method of capture has been determined. Your next step is the difficult choice of choosing the merchant service provider that will work best with the way your company operates. This should include but not be limited to the overall customer service, technical support, and how easy it is to reach and work with the customer service and technical support teams and, finally, how responsive they are. Does the company provide a designated sales representative and, if so, how accessible is this representative? Are contracts required? If so, for how long and what penalties would be enforced if the contract is broken? Are gift and loyalty programs also offered? Is the company accredited or affiliated with any reputable associations? What, if any, are the other miscellaneous fees (statement, service, and PCI)? Last, but certainly not least, what kind of pricing programs does the company offer?

Before choosing the company based solely on "rate" it is important that you first understand how and for what the business is being charged when accepting any type of card. You will incur fees with this service; however, knowing why is very important. The pricing system that rates are based upon is extremely complex. Shopping for the lowest introduction rate does not necessarily mean that you will have received the best overall deal for your company. The fact is that it could cost the business hundreds, if not thousands, of dollars annually or even monthly if the merchant neglects to look at all of the possible charges that can and will be incurred. Beware of the representative who only tries to sell the lowest rate!

Merchant service card transactions are cleared and settled by acquiring banks with the issuing banks through a system called Interchange. The system also regulates the rates and fees for the different types of cards that customers carry. These rates and fees are set by Visa or Master Card for all merchant service providers to base their pricing. The best way to explain this is by comparing the rate for a debit or check card issued by a bank that is used as a Visa or MasterCard during a purchase to a special rewards card that someone might be using to accumulate extra bonus miles to redeem free or discounted items. Customers will use these cards and it is virtually impossible for the merchant to know what type of card is being presented until your statement is received. It is equally as important to understand that keyed-in transactions or e-commerce transactions will be charged at a higher cost based on this same Interchange price structure.

Imagine the following example: Using simple math, a $100 purchase at a retail store that might only cost the merchant $1.50 if a debit or check card is used could cost more than $5.00 in some cases depending on what pricing program the business chose, if a rewards card is used for that exact same purchase. If that same purchase is done via the Internet or is keyed in, the merchant might pay $2.75 for one type of card or more than $5.00 in some cases depending on which price program the merchant accepted for another card. These additional charges are typically known as Mid-Qualified transactions and Non-Qualified transactions.

Remember that the card companies are constantly advertising and marketing to consumers to obtain and use their cards when they purchase rather than using cash or a check. Having the logos in the window, counter, flyer, website, etc. helps attract consumers. Accepting cards as a method of payment reduces dealing with receivables 30, 60, 90, or 120 days old. Promoting gift cards allows your company to receive payment prior to even selling the goods and services by providing certain incentives. Promoting loyalty cards help to entice consumers to purchase more of your product on a regular basis. Both provide additional marketing and company brand recognition that will help increase your customer base as well as help retain existing customers. Government benefits are paid by issuing EBT cards in lieu of paper checks and food stamps.

As shown, there is much more than meets the eye with this complicated pricing structure. Understand exactly how your business will be capturing the payments and who your customers are. Talk to your representative about all of the services not just the price structure. Make sure that charges will be clearly identified in the monthly statements. Don't be afraid to ask these questions. Most importantly, grow your business by concentrating on what you do best without fear of the merchant service provider's invoices, knowing that you have successfully addressed the items in this chapter.

Chapter 11

Cash-Flow Tips For Your Business

By Vito Mazza

When a company provides a product or service, it has every right to expect to be paid on a timely basis. However, anyone who's been in business for just a month or more has already learned that prompt payment is not always the case. While customers and clients expect promptness and professionalism in regard to delivery of our products or services, somehow, they don't always adopt those same standards when it comes time to paying their bills!

Particularly in this economy, all businesses are interested in cutting costs and IMPROVING CASH FLOW! Accounts not paid within your terms can have a dramatically negative impact on your "cash flow." Unfortunately, we have all witnessed recently that the very survival of many businesses has been placed in jeopardy over this critical issue. A "FOR LEASE" sign on storefronts and offices of previously long-term, local business is a sad result of not taking care of one's Account Receivables in a professional and timely way. The irony that this is CHAPTER 11 is certainly NOT lost on me, nor I trust on you! Here are some ideas that will help, if implemented:

1. **Have a Defined Credit or Collection Policy**

One of the major causes of overdue receivables is that the business has not explained to its customers and staff exactly when accounts are supposed to be paid. If customers are not clearly informed that their accounts are to be paid on time, then chances are they will pay late or, sometimes, not at all. Make sure that your terms of payment are clearly stated in writing to each customer. Being specific is very important. We encourage clients to use the concept of a *"date certain"* when talking about due dates and time. Instead of talking about payments being due in "10 Days" or "30 Days," give the actual date of July 9, 2016 - the *"date certain"* - so they don't have to figure out when 10 days or 30 days might actually be. Be diplomatic but be persistent.

2. **Invoice Promptly and Send Statements Regularly**

If you don't have a systematic invoicing and billing system, get one. Many times the customer hasn't paid simply because they haven't been billed or reminded to pay in a timely manner. This situation usually occurs in smaller or newer businesses where they may be short-handed on staff needed for timely invoicing and billing. If you don't have a systematic billing system, get one.

3. **Address Service Requested**

One of the most difficult collection problems is tracking down a customer who has "skipped." All businesses should be aware of a special service offered by the U.S. Postal Service. Any statement or correspondence sent out from a business or professional office should have the words **"Address Service Requested"** printed or stamped on the envelope typically just below your return address on the top left corner. If a statement or invoice is sent to a customer who has moved without informing you of their new address and the words "Address Service Requested" appear on the envelope, the Post Office will research this information and return the envelope to you on a yellow sticker that gives the new address or other updated information. If the customer has placed a "forwarding order" with the Post Office, the Post Office is required to forward the envelope to the customer and give you a Form #3547 with the new address. Currently, your business will be charged less than $1 per manual notice issued, a reasonable price to pay for your first level of "skip-tracing." This will keep your address files up to date.

4. **Contact Overdue Accounts More Frequently**

There is no law that says that you are only allowed to contact a customer once a month. The old adage "The squeaky wheel gets the grease" has a great deal of merit when it comes to collecting past due accounts. It's an excellent idea to contact slow and late payers every 7-14 days. Doing so will enable you to diplomatically remind the customer of your originally-stated terms of payment.

Automating and outsourcing your "1st party reminders" for a small flat fee is an excellent time-saver and recovery tool.

5. Use Your Aging Summary Report Not Your Feelings

Many well-meaning business owners and staff members have let an account age beyond the point of ever being collected because of the "feeling" that the customer would pay eventually. While there are isolated cases of unusual situations, the truth is that if you aren't being paid, someone else is. Stick to your systematic follow-up plan. You'll soon identify who really intends to pay and who doesn't. You can then take appropriate actions.

6. Make Sure Your Staff is Well-Trained

Even "experienced" staff members can sometimes become jaded when dealing with past due customers. This usually happens when debtors have broken previously made promises to pay their balance due. Make sure your staff is firm, yet courteous, when dealing with debtors. Your entire staff could benefit from customer service training because, in effect, they must "sell" your customers on the idea that you expect to be paid. Make sure that your collection staff is trained to bring the account to current status, while at the same time maintaining "good will" with your client base. Here is an example of the kind of training we offer our clients:

A Mini-Course on "HOW TO ASK FOR MONEY" - Asking for Money is a 3-Step Process!

Step One: Sympathize and show compassion. "I know how that happens sometimes." This diffuses any possible anger and may even catch them off guard.

Step Two: Restate the obligation. "Mr. Smith, you know that your account was originally due on mm/dd/yyyy."
This should cause some guilt on their behalf as well as have them realize you are "right" in asking to be paid.

DO NOT ASK: • "How much can you pay?" • "When can you pay?" • "Can you pay something?"
These questions give control of the conversation to the debtor, enabling them to give unreasonable answers.

Step Three: DO ASK: • "How Much Are You Short?" • "Mr. Smith, of the $200 that is owed, how much of the balance due are you short right now?"
1. If they can pay some of the amount due now, then give them a *"date certain"* to pay the balance.
2. If they are short the whole amount, you can still be in control to negotiate payment terms.

7. Admit Any Mistakes on Your Part and Correct Them As Soon As Possible

Sometimes customers don't pay because they feel that your bill contains an error or a mistake. If you have made a mistake, admit it and correct it quickly. Beware: Do not try and cover up mistakes! Most of your customers realize that mistakes can happen in business. Unfortunately, in today's difficult financial environment, many customers believe that as the owner or president or Doctor, you "don't need the money". Denying an obvious error only fans the fire of resentment that many of your customers may already be feeling today.

8. Follow all Federal (FDCPA) and State Collection Laws

Check out the entire THE FAIR DEBT COLLECTION PRACTICES ACT, revised in (2010) on the web at: http://1.usa.gov/19E4y8o. In many states, businesses are governed by the same collection laws that regulate collection agencies. For example, calling customers at an odd hour or disclosing to a third party that the debtor owes you money are just a couple of the numerous collection practices that can cause serious repercussions. If you're not sure, call your state's department of finance which governs and monitors collection agencies.

9. Use a Third Party Sooner

If you've systematically pursued your past due accounts for 60 to 90 days from the due date (and they still haven't paid), you're being delivered a message by your client. More than likely, you've requested payment four to six times in the form of phone calls, letters, and statements. Statistics show that after 90 days in-house collection efforts lose up to 80% of their effectiveness. That means that the time and financial resources budgeted for "in-house" collection efforts should be focused within the first 60 to 90 days, when the bulk of your accounts can and should be collected. From that point on a 3rd party can motivate your clients to pay you in ways that your staff simply cannot based solely upon the fact that the demand for payment is coming from someone other than you or your in-house (1st PARTY) team. This LEVERAGE is called the "POWER of 3rd PARTY INTERVENTION".

When to Seek a 3rd Party:
- Abuse of your written payment policies/procedures
- Broken promises, as in "the check is in the mail"
- Unable to reach by phone (voicemail, always in a meeting, answering service, etc.)
- Disconnected phone or phone number changed to unlisted
- Missed payments or payments getting smaller
- Certified mail returned "Unclaimed"
- Admission of inability to pay
- Debtor says "You will get paid when I get paid"
- Bounced check with no response to follow-up calls (DANGER: these depreciate rapidly!)
- Disputed balance or disputed quality of service or product
Before paying a contingency collection agency, an attorney, or using small claims court, we highly recommend that you explore the option of using "EARLY, DIPLOMATIC 3RD PARTY INTERVENTION" for a fixed flat-fee.

10. Remember That Nobody Collects Every Account

Even by setting up and adhering to a specific collection plan there may still be a few accounts that will never be collected. By utilizing early intervention and identifying these problem accounts, you will save yourself and your company a great deal of time and money. Even though a few may slip through, you will find that overall the number of slow paying and non-paying accounts will greatly diminish ... and that is a victory, in itself!

Chapter 12

Alternative Business Financing: Bridge Your Financial Gap

By Vivian C. Gaspar and Frank Gallipoli

Alternative financing might just be the most misunderstood phrase in lending among borrowers. Simply put, the phrase is used most often when conforming financing cannot be obtained through traditional means such as conventional bank lending programs. This would include how quickly the funds are required. Although many alternative financing programs, specifically sub-prime lending, have disappeared over the years due to the predatory lending laws, there are still many good financing options available for business owners. Whether there is a thriving or a downturn in the economy, these programs have been around for many years and can be of great assistance for business owners depending on the situation.

Forms of alternative lending can include asset-based lending such as accounts receivable financing also known as factoring programs, inventory and purchase order financing, cash flow loans, or merchant cash advance. Private and angel investors will also lend money for a specific business type or property. Choosing the program that works best for the business will depend mostly on broker funding resources, the business owner's due diligence, or both. It is important to understand all of the details of the financing program and exactly how it can and will benefit the business. The dumb question is the one that is not asked!

Historically, small businesses have always struggled to secure conventional bank financing loans. At times, being declined for a loan can be a degrading and humiliating experience. There are many different reasons why going the alternative financing route might, in some circumstances, be more advantageous to the business owner. Be it preference or necessity, funding terms, funding times, personal guarantees, amount required, credit issues, collateral, length of time in business, and terms or convenience are just a few reasons why this might be a better method of obtaining financing.

Interest rates are typically higher than what local banks will offer as core or introductory pricing products. On the flipside, underwriting guidelines and criteria are often much more flexible and easier for business owners to work with. Additionally, projects and loans can be funded in a much faster time period as well sometimes in as little as two business days. Some programs will allow monthly interest-only payments to be made over a specific period of time while other programs will fully amortize the loan. Again, it is important to know all of the terms and conditions of the loan including late payments and early payoff penalties, if any. Always make sure there is an exit strategy in place. Utilizing these resources can benefit a business in many ways. For the most part, alternative lenders do not place restrictions on the use of funds. Business owners can utilize these programs for all different reasons. Many have outstanding receivable issues and need the working capital to meet payroll, expand inventory, pay debt or taxes, address emergency repairs, manage unexpected operating expenses, or expand and remodel the facility. Maybe the business wants to do some additional advertising and marketing to promote the company and products. Some are just trying to overcome seasonality or cyclicality. Others don't want to risk personal assets and prefer not to sign personal guarantees.

Unlike traditional lending, alternative financing programs do not solely determine approvals based on credit scores, income, and financials. These programs also factor into consideration many aspects of the business such as cash-flow volume, receivables, inventory, and the type of business making funds easier to obtain. Certain businesses that have recently been declined for a loan from a traditional lender might find funds readily available from an alternative source because of this.

These programs are not for everyone but can and have helped millions of businesses around the world achieve their goals. They can provide simple solutions to assist a business and should not be discounted.

These programs will assist and address the specific monetary needs of the company allowing the owners to concentrate on running the business rather than worrying about keeping the doors open or slowing the business growth due to lack of financing.

Chapter 13

Getting Paid Promptly in the Construction Business

By Douglas A. Goldstein, Esq.

If you are a construction contractor, you probably worry about getting paid on time. After all, you need cash-flow to cover ongoing labor and material costs.

Under New Jersey's Prompt Payment Act (the "Act") (N.J.S.A. 2A:30A-1 & -2), in addition to the amount owed under the contract, a prime contractor may be entitled to interest at a rate of prime plus 1% and reasonable attorneys' fees and costs, if:

• the contractor performs (in New Jersey) according to its contract with the owner (such as a landlord, developer, or homeowner);

• the contractor provides written notice to the owner of the work performed and requests payment pursuant to what the contract entitles the contractor;

• within 30 days after the agreed upon billing date, and if the owner has "approved and certified" the billing for the work, the owner does not pay the amount due under the contract.

(With the exception of certain public entities, the owner is deemed to have "approved and certified" the billing for the work if, after 20 days after the owner receives the contractor's written notice, the owner does not respond with a written statement of the amount withheld from payment and why.)

• the contract permits a party to resort to alternative dispute resolution (such as arbitration) to resolve a payment dispute; and

• the contractor successfully prosecutes a lawsuit in New Jersey to collect the amount owed under the Act.

The Act also may permit the contractor, after giving 7 day's written notice, to suspend performance under the contract if the owner (1) has not made the payment required by the Act; (2) has not provided the required written response; and (3) is not engaged in a good faith effort to resolve the reason for the withholding.

Beware: The Act will not restrict the rights and remedies of a residential homeowner or purchaser with respect to the property being improved. A homeowner facing a lawsuit under the Act might try to assert a counterclaim under the many consumer protection laws including the Consumer Fraud Act (a topic I will cover in a future article).

You should consult with an attorney before taking matters into your own hands. My suggestions are not intended to provide legal advice on any matter, are provided for informational purposes only, should not be used as a substitute for the retention of legal counsel in your state, might not reflect the latest legal developments, should be viewed at your own risk, and are provided on an as is basis. You should not act or refrain from acting based on any information contained in this article.

Chapter 14

3 Attributes Your Next Financial Advisor Must Have

By Brian T. Cody, CFP

There's an old expression that goes "inspect what you expect" and that expression certainly applies to watching your portfolio. The best way to find out if you're working with the wrong advisor is follow the money.

The biggest issue I see when someone comes to me after having a bad experience with a financial advisor is that they didn't ask their financial advisor what he or she was getting paid while selling them a product. Certainly, you will want your financial advisor to make a living at his job. However, it has to be fair. Some advisors provide products or services that have high upfront fees. Two of the important aspects you need to be aware of are if the products or services have upfront fees and what are the fees and, secondly, what exactly is the advisor's incentive for this advisor to continue servicing you once he has bought you these products.

Another way to see if you're with the wrong advisor is by asking your advisor what they have done to educate themselves over the last two years. Have they attended any seminars or earned new certifications? All of us must constantly be sharpening our knowledge base to keep up with changes in technology, the markets, and regulations. Your advisor should be a life-long student.

Finally, a good way to determine if you are with the wrong advisor is to see how they treat you. If they don't return your phone calls in a timely manner, if they don't smile when they see you and express a strong desire to help you, you are probably with the wrong advisor.

Five attributes for a great financial advisor to replace the wrong advisor:

1. Look for somebody that is a Certified Financial Planner TM (CFP®) or a Chartered Financial Consultant® (ChFC®) – these are two of the toughest certifications to receive in the industry.

2. Look for person that has been in the industry for at least 5 years. There certainly are great financial advisors who have been in the industry for a shorter period of time; however, since so many finance advisors fail out within the first five years, don't take the chance that you're going to be with the person that is not going to survive.

3. Look for an advisor who has been referred to you by somebody else. It's always good to have somebody else refer any professional. First, the referrer has vetted the advisor and second, the advisor has to provide you good service or he will look bad in front of two clients.

4. Find an advisor that's going to give you a plan. Before you have to pay anything, ask the advisor to tell you how your money is going to be invested, what's the likelihood of reward and risk, and how does it fit into the overall picture for your financial needs.

5. Try to work with a financial advisor that is with a reputable company. You're investing your hard-earned money with this financial advisor and you would hope that there be a solid organization backing your financial advisor's practice.

Chapter 15

Mediation for Business Owners

By Robert J. McDonnell, MS APM

"Discourage litigation. Persuade your neighbors to compromise whenever you can."

— Abraham Lincoln

When a conflict or disagreement arises in business or business relationships, today's business owners are realizing that mediation can play a helpful role in resolving their situation. Whether the issue in dispute is a contract, an employer-employee relationship, or other matter, mediation is becoming popular as an easier, generally quicker, and less expensive way to move ahead.

That is because:

- Parties maintain privacy and control over the outcome of the dispute
- The process is informal and inexpensive. Attorneys may or may not be required to participate
- It is a non-adversarial approach
- The process encourages creative solutions
- Mediation can preserve and enhance relationships while setting guidelines for future relationships
- Mediation eliminates magnification of disputes which often accompanies costly litigation

What is Mediation?

Mediation is a process that provides for trained third-party neutrals to facilitate communication and negotiation among parties in order to help resolve current and ongoing disputes. By helping parties change the quality of their conflict interaction from negative and destructive to positive and constructive, the mediator facilitates the parties to make their decisions together based on an understanding of their own views, the other's views, and the situation they face. Because mediation is non-adversarial it is very different than litigation.

Mediation is rapidly becoming a popular and successful form of dispute resolution. Through the confidential process individuals in conflict are provided with the opportunity to make better choices in the face of conflict and interpersonal differences leading to more informed, satisfying, and lasting resolutions. Not only can the actual dispute be resolved but mediation offers the opportunity for the participants to overcome misunderstandings and misperceptions and to restore trust and respect in their working relationship. At the same time, the problem solving and negotiation skills applied, developed, and learned in mediation can be used by participants to help resolve future disputes.

The most important prerequisite for a successful mediation is the willingness of the parties to resolve the disagreement. Mediation has a statistically high success rate and participants report greater satisfaction with the process and the outcome than in traditional litigation including arbitration.

There are typically two main areas of business relationships where mediation works effectively. In the first, parties have a dispute and need to have financial resolution of the matter and move on separately. These instances involve positional bargaining where each party wants a large "piece of the pie" as possible. The second is where there is an ongoing relationship and there will be business transactions or personal interactions in the future. These may include an employee/employer or supplier/client relationship or possibly a business partnership.

In the situations where there is an ongoing relationship, mediation can be particularly beneficial. A mediator can assist with joint problem solving and help parties develop non-legal more elegant solutions for their mutual gain. Often, this aids in preserving the relationship.

Both individuals and businesses in litigation experience costs that are quite real, yet are often unseen. There are obvious costs associated with litigation such as attorney costs, filing fees, depositions, discovery, etc. There are also unseen costs that come with litigation including lost productivity, time spent managing or participating in the various aspects of litigation, as well as emotional costs.

Basically, any dispute can be mediated including those civil disputes involving contracts, leases, small business ownership, employment, and others. Non-violent criminal matters such as claims of verbal or other personal harassment can also be successfully mediated.

Although there are hundreds of thousands of laws on the books, many types of common disputes simply do not raise a legal claim that you can take to court. These can include disputes between family members, employees, or neighbors. Fortunately, mediation is available even when courts are not.

As an example, a successful family-owned business may be struggling with the issues that arise as the founder/owner looks to pass on ownership and/or control of the business. There may be varying levels of interest among the family members who feel they are entitled to or expected to come into ownership of the business. Mediation can provide the parties with a safe, non-threatening process that would address the underlying interests and concerns of the parties and, with their agreement, assist the family in addressing the issues. Clearly, the family is interested in maintaining both the business and the family relationships both of which could be negatively impacted by protracted adversarial litigation.

Understanding the process. What makes the process "Mediation?"

Successful mediation, as an alternative method of dispute resolution, has the following elements:

1. **An impartial third party**

The third-party neutral makes the entire process work. As long as there is a neutral facilitator, the parties can trust that they have safety in the process.

2. **A third-party who protects the integrity of the process**

Not only does the mediator not take sides against any party to the mediation, the mediator does not usurp the parties' rights to disclose or not disclose information. The mediator preserves the integrity of the proceedings.

3. **Good faith from the participants**

Good faith includes not only entering into mediation with the intent to work towards a resolution, it also includes not using the process for outside purposes. Both the behavior and integrity of the neutral party are important in creating and preserving good faith.

4. **The presence of the parties**

Obviously, the parties to the dispute need to be present. Those with full authority to act for the parties must attend so that the parties can work towards resolution.

5. **An appropriate site or venue**

Generally, this means a site that is conducive to the process. The location must be one where neutrality, confidentiality, and inclusiveness can be maintained.

6. **Confidentiality**

In many states, the discussions during mediation sessions are confidential to the extent agree upon by the parties or as provided for by other law or rule of the state. In most cases, parties expect that communications during mediation will not be discussed with others outside the mediation. Parties may even choose mediation to resolve the dispute to assure privacy of their issues.

<u>Opting for Mediation</u>:

Business owners in a dispute should consider suggesting mediation as a means for resolving the dispute. Parties in mediation have to agree to be there so the first step is agreeing on a mediator. The parties can each provide proposed mediators and then mutually agree on the mediator.

Competent mediators come for a variety of professions and employ different styles. When choosing mediators, consider experience, reputation, training, profession, accreditation, and/or certification. Consult with other business owners, attorneys, state ADR (Alternate Dispute Resolution) organizations, or state and national mediation organizations or associations.

Helpful advice for business owners in a conflict:

Don't litigate... mediate.

Chapter 16

Employment Law Facts

By Marc Garbar, Esq.

Caveat: As employment law differs from state to state, this chapter is intended to provide general information regarding general employment practices. Please speak with an attorney in your state if you seek further information regarding employment law. Nothing in this chapter is intended to provide or should be relied upon as legal advice. Nothing in this chapter is intended to cause an attorney/client relationship between author and reader.

Who is Affected by Employment Law?

Seemingly anyone and everyone associated with a business (i.e. the owners, managers, supervisors, and all other employees). Of course, the business itself, no matter how small or large, so long as it has employees, is greatly affected. Employment law cases can cripple or even bankrupt businesses; can significantly impact an individual's career (recall how it affected Herman Cain's 2012 presidential bid); and can also cause substantial employment turmoil.

As previously mentioned in the caveat, employment law differs from state to state. This is important as without state or local anti-discrimination laws, only businesses with fifteen or more employees are impacted by the general (federal) laws. Those laws include Title VII (which includes anti-discrimination provisions affecting race, color, religion, national origin, and sex (which includes gender, sexual harassment, and pregnancy), the Age Discrimination in Employment Act, the Americans with Disabilities Amendments Act and a number of others. A significant class of individuals which is not protected under any of the federal anti-discrimination laws is sexual orientation. Sexual orientation may be protected under state or local laws.

By way of example, we need look no further than the vast differences between New York and New Jersey law. While many laws in both states are similar, the laws of employment are on completely different spectrums. Both states are considered at-will employment states meaning an employee can be terminated for good reason, bad reason, or no reason, so long as the employer is not in violation of any of the anti-discrimination/retaliation laws, is non-union, and a written contract of employment with the employee does not exist. However, the similarities end there. The anti-discrimination laws in New York require only four employees to be applicable. The strength of the law pales in comparison to federal law which is why, for the most part, attorneys in New York will not represent employees against employers with less than fifteen employees. The only exception to that principal is if the discrimination occurred in New York City (which encompasses the five boroughs of Manhattan, Queens, the Bronx, Brooklyn, and Staten Island) as New York City has its own anti-discrimination statute (the New York City Administrative Code) which has significant teeth. On the flip side, the New Jersey anti-discrimination statute is so significant, practitioners in New Jersey consider it malpractice to bring a discrimination claim under any of the federal laws as the law in New Jersey requires only one or more employees and also allows for unlimited punitive damages (the federal law has a sliding scale of capped punitive damages and New York State does not offer any punitive damages for employment discrimination). Undoubtedly, navigating the laws in New York, New Jersey, or any other state requires consultation with an attorney who is not only licensed to practice in whichever state is impacted but who also understands this area of the law.

How to Avoid Employment Law Issues Altogether

The best and most effective way to avoid employment law issues is to take them on head on! For starters, an employee manual or personnel policies and procedures should be prepared and provided to all employees. The two most important parts of that multi-page document are: 1) the pages which discuss anti-discrimination/harassment policies which includes the mechanisms to follow if an employee believes he/she has a complaint of discrimination or harassment; and 2) the detachable page of the document on which the employee signs his/her name to state that the employee manual or personnel policies and procedures has been received. That detachable page is placed inside the personnel file of the employee in which it shall forever remain for safe-keeping. If the above steps occur, the employer is more than half-way there.

The next big step is for the employer to train its supervisory/management employees on what to do when a complaint is communicated. It is one thing to have the employee manual or personnel policies and procedures. It is another to make certain that supervisory/management employees follow it! For a smaller business, the business owner may be the only supervisor or manager. Depending upon the state and the number of employees employed by the business, the business could face liability. If liability is an issue, the business owner, managers, and supervisors need to know and understand what procedures must be followed in the event of a complaint which can be made in writing sent by email, transmitted by text, or communicated verbally. In essence, to avoid or limit its liability, the employer should: 1) maintain and distribute sexual harassment/discrimination policies and procedures to all of its employees; 2) follow its own policies when a complaint is made; and 3) investigate and take prompt, remedial measures in response to a complaint of harassment/discrimination.

Before any complaints are filed by an employee, and starting from the time an employee is hired, the employer has to begin the process of complete protection and insulation. This is done through one simple step which, similar to location in the real estate industry, must be stated three times: "Document, document, document." Now that it's been said, make sure it occurs. If an employee is constantly late for work – document it. If an employee is not performing in an effective manner – document it. Whatever it is, and whatever is going on, be sure everything is documented. Two examples will illustrate why:

Example 1: The pregnant employee

Company ABC employed Mary. Mary worked for ABC for several years. During that time, she was constantly late, performed deficiently in her work, etc. ABC, for the most part, let those issues go. A supervisor of ABC may have verbally spoken with her once or twice regarding lateness or work deficiency, but the supervisor does not remember when, and nothing was ever documented.

Finally, ABC decided enough was enough. Mary's lateness was out of control, as was her work performance. So ABC decided to terminate Mary. But just one problem exists – Mary is now pregnant.

Had ABC been documenting Mary's lateness and work deficiencies all along, termination shouldn't be a problem, regardless of Mary's pregnancy. She most likely would have already been warned in writing. When it occurred again, regardless of Mary's protected employment law status, ABC would have every right to act in accordance with its warning document. However, because ABC was not documenting, it is probably stuck with Mary for a long time – not only throughout the pregnancy, but for a significant time thereafter.

Example 2: Inconsistent action by the employer

Employee George, who is African-American, and Employee Robert, who is Caucasian, both have similar backgrounds, experience, and years working for the employer. George was not as productive of an employee as Robert and was often deficient in his performance.

A financial blunder occurred which caused the employer significant loss. Both Robert and George were equally responsible. However, because George was the allegedly deficient employee, he was the only one who was terminated. Robert remained at the job with a verbal warning. George sued the employer for discrimination, i.e., for treating him differently than a similarly-situated employee based on his race.

With well-documented personnel files, the employer could more easily defend its actions by pointing to the stark differences in the employment history of the two employees. However, without documentation, which would have included prior written warnings to George, the employer would have a very difficult time justifying its inconsistent employment decision to terminate the African-American employee, but not the Caucasian employee, for the same infraction.

The above examples illustrate why it is so important to document all adverse and questionable employee activity. While documentation may be somewhat burdensome, that burden pales in comparison to the financial tragedy which is just around the corner in the event the employer is hit with a lawsuit. Attorneys' fees could cost an employer hundreds of thousands of dollars to defend an employment discrimination case and that amount will be due and payable even if the employer wins. If the employee wins, the employer could be responsible for back pay, front pay, compensatory damages, and punitive damages. Additionally, due to fee-shifting under the federal law, the employer could also be responsible to pay the employee's attorneys' fees. When comparing the administrative burden against effectively being forced out of business or paying a million dollar judgment, clearly, the burdensome steps, to the extent they are burdensome at all, must be followed.

Think Resolution

An employer can handle anticipated employment adversity (discrimination or harassment complaints) by either resolving them, litigating them, or a combination of both. While the first option – resolution – generally makes sense, there might be times, albeit rare ones, when an employer may want to "make an example" of an employee. This occurs when an employer wants other employees to see the complaining employee have his/her clock turned upside down by the employer's attorneys so that the other employees will think twice before rendering their own complaints. For the most part, I generally advise employers to resolve employment disputes quickly and effectively. The best and most effective way to achieve such success is through use of a great, strategic tool – the severance agreement.

Severance agreements are effective because they offer employees something which employees would not otherwise be entitled to receive, i.e., additional compensation (pay, benefits, or both) subsequent to the cessation of employment from the company. In exchange, the employer receives the employee's signature to the agreement which includes, more importantly than anything else, the employee's release of all claims against the employer. It most often also includes confidentiality and non-disparagement provisions as well as other employee restrictions. The key question for the employer is what to offer in such an agreement for the employee to say "I do." How much to offer in the severance agreement is generally case specific and is best decided following consultation with an attorney.

Severance agreements, when prepared correctly by an attorney, soon become the employer's best friend as they allow the employer to sleep at night. Without such an agreement, the employer, when faced with a difficult employment issue, has to constantly wonder will this be the day that a complaint is filed in court. With a correctly prepared and executed agreement, a very troubled employer can soon become a relaxed one.

Conclusion

Bottom line: Employment law is a complicated area which should be discussed with attorneys in the field if/when you believe you finally want to protect your business from a number of the pitfalls discussed above or if you believe that an employment matter presently exists. If it is the holiday season, and you want to take extreme measures of protection, please read the attached article which I recently published:

DON'T SING THE BLUES THIS HOLIDAY SEASON AND DON'T SERVE ALCOHOL AT YOUR BUSINESS HOLIDAY PARTIES.

Fifty weeks is a long time. Fifty weeks of seeing the same people, day in and day out. The same people that you spend a lot more time with than you do with your own families. The same people that for hopefully two weeks of the year you don't have to see while you are on vacation. Fifty two weeks ago, you celebrated the holiday season with your business colleagues. This year, assuming the business can still afford to have a party, the most important thing to remember is to have the party without the alcohol.

As an employment law attorney, I hope that some of you do not take my advice. If everyone took my advice, I would be unemployed. There is a reason why January is my busiest month, every year, and that reason can be summed up in one word – alcohol. Alcohol that is served at holiday parties in December leads business owners, managers, supervisors, and employees to engage in activities that are frowned upon in the work place – fraternization.

Conversations at the water cooler about American Idol, the presidential election, the economy, and what's being served at your home on Thanksgiving is fair game. It doesn't help the Employer's pocketbook when time is wasted at the water cooler but at least it keeps everyone in stable enough condition to deal with the daily stresses at work. But when you take away the water cooler and substitute it with a keg, bottles of foreign wine, and other distilled spirits, American Idol becomes "can I give you a lift home". The economy becomes pornography and "what's being served on Thanksgiving" becomes "I am leaving my wife for you…I promise."

What had been a vanilla clean work environment has now turned into a landmine of litigation. Sexual harassment and/or gender discrimination law suits can be extremely costly for businesses, business owners, supervisors, managers, and employees. Everyone is fair game in the litigation battle and everyone can be spending their days in court instead of behind their desks. What can you do to control this craziness or possibly avoid it all together? Here are a few simple ways to keep your business running or to keep your job:

If you are a business owner or a decision maker regarding the festivities:

- Don't serve alcohol

- Conduct the party on your business premises if you can so that it is in a controlled environment and your employees will act more respectfully.

- Serve some great food

- Use the party as a platform to motivate the troops and get everyone psyched and ready for next year

- Inform everyone at the party about the bonuses (if you can afford to pay any) that will be paid in the next paycheck and thank everyone for a great year and a job well done.

- Speak with a party planner to come up with some fun corporate ideas that are rated nothing more than PG.

If you are a supervisor, manager, or employed in any human resources type activity:

- Don't drink any alcohol or keep it to a bare minimum

- Try to avoid conversations with anyone at the office that you do not normally speak with on a recurrent basis especially if you find that person very attractive.

- If you are romantically involved with anyone at the office, and it is a secret, this is not a good time to do anything but keep your distance. With possible impaired judgment, you may say or do something that you will very soon regret.

- Avoid private and personal conversations with anyone in a dark corner. Keep your conversations fun and lively but keep them at the table or at the bar and try to be professional.

If you are an employee with limited supervisory or managerial responsibilities, if any:

- You are the most fungible, so do your best to not be the one that is being talked about at the water cooler the next day

- To avoid being the one talked about at the water cooler the next day, try to avoid alcohol as much as you can. If you are invited to share a drink or toast with a supervisor,, accept, but nurse it as much as possible.

- Don't grow beer or wine muscles and approach the business owner or higher up to tell him/her ways that you can improve their business. If you have a great business idea, bring it to the right person on any other day of the year. There are plenty of days to choose from.

- Don't show off either your mass eating or mass drinking skills. This is the time to be conservatively social not the life of the party.

- And finally, if you are on the prowl, wait until after the party is over to go hunting and do your hunt at a very different location. Hopefully, someone else at a different party on the other side of town is reading this same article and perhaps that person will also be hunting or be available at a local tavern or club near you.

All in all, it's holiday time! So long as you think of holiday time at the workplace as anything but "party time" and avoid all of the potential pitfalls and landmines that have been categorized above, you can make it through this holiday season and still be earning a living come the first of the year. Happy holidays to all! I hope to not hear from you in January (but I won't be taking vacation just in case).

Chapter 17

New Jersey's Consumer Fraud Act – What Is a Consumer?

By Douglas A. Goldstein, Esq.

Picture this: A company, Onyx Acceptance, makes a "guaranteed reservation" at Trump Taj Mahal Casino Resort in Atlantic City ("Trump") for a banquet hall and 60 guest rooms and prepaid $29,754.05. Unfortunately, Trump over-books and cannot honor the full reservation and, instead, after several hours of arguing, attempts to remedy the situation by booking rooms at area hotels and providing free transportation back and forth. As a result, Onyx deems the event a failure and the matter heads to court.

New Jersey's Consumer Fraud Act was intended to protect the public against unscrupulous contractors and others. A claim for relief under the Act requires a showing of:

- "unlawful conduct" by the defendant;

- "an ascertainable loss" by the plaintiff; and

- a causal connection between the defendant's unlawful conduct and the plaintiff's ascertainable loss.

At trial, the court concluded that Trump falsely represented the guaranteed nature of Onyx's rooms which constituted an "unconscionable business practice" in violation of the Consumer

Fraud Act. For purposes of the Consumer Fraud Act it did not matter if Trump acted in good faith. "When Trump represented that the rooms were guaranteed, Trump did not really mean that the rooms would be guaranteed, at least not in the way any reasonable consumer would understand because Trump defined the term guaranteed in a way that no reasonable consumer could predict."

The end result? After an appeal, Onyx was awarded $212,159.74 consisting of $89,262.15 in treble damages (three times the underlying damage award of $29,754.05) plus $90,000 in counsel fees and costs of $32,897.59.

The house does not always win and the Consumer Fraud Act is not limited to individuals.

You should consult with an attorney before taking matters into your own hands. My suggestions are not intended to provide legal advice on any matter, are provided for informational purposes only, should not be used as a substitute for the retention of legal counsel in your state, might not reflect the latest legal developments, should be viewed at your own risk, and are provided on an as-is basis. You should not act, or refrain from acting, based on any information contained in this article.

Chapter 18

Being Preferred Is Not Always a Good Thing

By Douglas A. Goldstein, Esq.

What if immediately after a customer pays you for a service or product you provided the customer files for bankruptcy relief? You might consider yourself fortunate for not being one of the customer's other creditors who might have to wait years before they recover possibly pennies on the dollar. But before you celebrate, take note: the bankruptcy estate could demand that you repay that money even if there was no dispute concerning the quality of your products or services.

Why should you have to return any money? Subject to certain exceptions, a bankruptcy trustee may seek to "avoid" or recover so-called "preferential transfers" if the debtor (here, the customer) made payment to a creditor (in this case, you):

- On account of a debt owed by the debtor before such transfer was made (such as a payment made on credit);

- On or within 90 days before the filing of the bankruptcy;

- While the debtor was insolvent (which is presumed during that 90-day period); and

- Enabling the creditor to receive more than the creditor would receive if the bankruptcy case were a liquidation and if the payment had not otherwise been made.

The rationale behind a preference action is that a creditor should not be "preferred" over other creditors. By bringing into the bankruptcy estate the monies paid to preferred creditors, the funds can be redistributed to all creditors. This might sound fair especially if a "preferred" creditor was paid ahead of other creditors only because it threatened the debtor's business or harassed its employees with aggressive collection tactics. But not all creditors fit this mold. For example, a creditor may get paid quickly because it offers a discount for early payment or is the only remaining supplier willing to sell to the debtor.

Either way, a preference lawsuit could spell disaster for a business if it must return a large preference payment. Remember, you still had to pay your employees and cover the cost of the materials that went into the goods and services that you provided.

Here are a few strategies to help minimize the risk of (or deal with) a preference lawsuit:

1. Do not extend much credit to a customer before confirming its creditworthiness. Your due diligence may avoid a credit sale that otherwise could lead to a preference lawsuit (or the more obvious result: nonpayment by a customer that is not creditworthy).

2. Take and perfect a security interest in the goods that you sell. If you can be made whole by repossessing the goods, such that the payment will not improve your position, the payment might not be recoverable as a preference.

3. Determine if you have a defense the most common of which being:

    a. The "contemporaneous exchange" defense (i.e. a C.O.D. sale).

    b. The "ordinary course of business" defense. Did the debtor incur, in the ordinary course of its business, the debt for which the debtor made the payment and either make the payment in the ordinary course of its and your business or financial affairs or according to ordinary business terms? Said differently, was the debt, the payment, and the surrounding events typical or unusual for all parties involved?

c. The "subsequent new value" defense. After the debtor made the payment to you did you provide more goods or services?

Each defense may depend on other factors and require complex analyses not discussed here.

4. Seek a properly worded guaranty, and indemnification, from a third party capable of protecting your claim.

These strategies might not guarantee a favorable outcome but they are a good starting point to protect yourself.

The bankruptcy law is complex so you should consult with an attorney before taking matters into your own hands. My suggestions are not intended to provide legal advice on any matter, are provided for informational purposes only, should not be used as a substitute for the retention of legal counsel in your state, might not reflect the latest legal developments, should be viewed at your own risk, and are posted on an as-is basis. You should not act, or refrain from acting, based on any information contained in this article.

Chapter 19

Vision, Leadership, and Strategy: Along the Path to Building Your Business Success

By Donna Price

Vision, leadership and strategy are the three essentials to building a thriving and successful business. Without these keys in place it is difficult, if not impossible, to move a business forward.

Why do we need a vision for our organization?

Many business owners feel that their organization is too small to need a clear and compelling vision but vision is what draws you to the future. It lays down the framework for moving forward. Leaders and business owners are the ones responsible for creating a powerful and compelling vision of the future. Maybe you haven't thought about what your vision for your company is or maybe you have lost sight of your original dream. What was that dream? Why did you start a company of your own or buy a company? This isn't the financial goal but what the company or business looks like down the road. If you are a sole proprietor or small business owner, do you see your company growing? Could there be a team someday? Does the vision involve expansion or a new building, new products, or services? Did you dream of creating the best business in the area, in the region, in the state or country? What did that look like?

A clear and compelling vision that inspires, drawing you into the future…like a magnet.

Visions should be written down and be compelling. Don't write down the numbers or finances but write down what it looks like, sounds like, feels like. What do you see in the future? When you write a vision statement it should be written in the present tense, as if it is happening now. You are living it now. It should be detailed and inspiring. To get to inspiration it has to tap into your senses and your emotions. So what does it sound like, feel like, look like, smell like, taste like? Put as much detail as possible into the vision. Spend time writing your vision. Make it clear, compelling, and inspiring. It becomes a magnet that draws you into the future. Successful businesses have a vision, the owner knows where he or she is going, and the staff is there with them. The vision pulls them into the future because everyone is invested in it and all are excited about it. Vision helps to keep you focused on the things you need to focus on. Explore your company vision. Take time to create a compelling vision story that inspires and gives you the road map for moving on to strategy.

Identify your "Core Purpose" – What you do every day.

Your Core Purpose is at the center of your business. It is the core of your business. What is your core purpose? Why do you do what you do? Often the core purpose is deeper than just what you do. Perhaps it is to be the friendliest or the cleanest or the best away from home experience. Often there is a story behind the core purpose that is what started the business or why you got into the business in the first place. Exploring your core purpose gives you information about how to craft your business. If your purpose is to give each person that comes to your business a unique experience, then that begins to help you determine how to design your business. If you are a restaurateur, perhaps a unique experience would be to affect the atmosphere, the menu, dress code, and perhaps even how people are greeted.

At the core of each business is the inner purpose...the deep essence...the heart.

Being unclear of your core purpose can result in being off course. You can be distracted and involve yourself and your business in operations that are not in alignment with your core. Are you clear what your business core purpose is? What is at the heart of your business?

Leaders guide the business.

Leaders see the future and envision it. The manager is responsible for the day-to-day operations but the leader creates the future. In your organization, you might play both of these roles but be clear that they are very different. The leaders create the vision - what will the company look like down the road. The vision is detailed with all elements included: how, what, why, when, where, and who. The vision is shared with the community – the staff, the customers, the vendors, and whomever is appropriate for your organization. Communicating the vision brings people to you. The leaders communicate the vision in a positive and a compelling language that includes the community. The staff should be interested in seeing how they fit into the vision.

Leaders see the future, envision it, and communicate it to everyone.

This is important because leaders want their own personal vision to fit into the company's vision. That's what keeps them coming to work and motivated for work. As the leader, you are also interested in knowing what the vision of your staff is. You may be able to help them achieve their personal vision within your organization.

Spend time with your staff talking about your vision for the company and finding out about their vision of the future. Perhaps they see themselves most successful in a different position. Maybe their goals are to one day own their own business. What a great opportunity for you, as leader, to mentor a motivated staff member.

The leaders move the vision forward to fulfill your purpose.

Vision of the leaders and vision of the staff lead to great success.

Do values impact our vision or purpose?

Values are critical. They are the foundation on which you make decisions. They guide you. It is vital that you have thought about the values of your company and organization. Write them down and tell your staff. Again, communication is important. If you value customer service, the staff needs to know this. They need to understand what it looks like and what it means. Or, perhaps, you have a value of integrity? Again, you need to communicate and teach it. What does integrity mean? What does it mean in your organization and how is it implemented? How does this help you in building your business?

Operating a business that is on a solid foundation is ready for development and growth. As you build your business and grow, you already know what your foundation is and how it guides the decisions you are making. Your vision and purpose also are components of your foundation.

Values are the foundation for making decisions and guide you in the direction that is in alignment with you and your company.

How do I incorporate strategy?

Once you have created a strong foundation you can create effective strategy. Strategy should be clear and focused on the top priorities for the organization. Begin by looking at all of the different areas in your organization or all of the different hats that you are wearing. What are the different areas of focus?

Core areas of focus may include the following:

- Operations
- Administration
- Finance
- Customer Service
- Program Operations
- Product Development
- Research and Development
- Marketing
- Public Relations
- Service Delivery

Your company probably does not include all of these or maybe some and perhaps different ones. What are the important strategies for each area of your company that you need to have happen in the next year to create the vision you have set? What are the goals for each area to create success?

Write your goals for each area of focus and make sure that they are clear and measurable. Measurable means that you can count it. It either happened, did not happen, or you can count the level at which it occurred. You might have a long list of goals. Pick the most important ones! Prioritize and then focus on those goals.

Clear and measurable goals for each area of focus moves your organization forward.

How do I make it happen? I have a plan and goals but I just don't seem to be able to make them happen.

The biggest problem that business owners have is making the plan happen. Many owners have great strategy and maybe even great vision. We see them fall short on implementation and communication - two keys to success.

Build in accountability. We are all great at making the list but we are not as good at making it happen. Create a plan for accountability. As a coach, I recommend coaching but it's not solely because I am a coach. I believe in coaching because it has worked for me and I see it work for my clients. Why does coaching work? It works because it holds us accountable. Once you have created a clear and compelling vision and a clear and measurable strategy, develop a system of accountability. There are several ways to do this:

- Hire a coach
- Create a mastermind group – a group of entrepreneurs that meet monthly or bi-weekly to report on their goals and hold each other accountable.
- Set up charts to track your goals.
- Meet as a leadership team or management team and create a performance culture that tracks and measures success.

Building in a system of accountability keeps you focused and on track for achieving your goals and vision.

Building in accountability is a key to success. There exists a gap in performance between strategy and implementation. Building in regular accountability meetings, at least monthly, fosters both performance and communication. Results improve and success increases. There is richness in collaborating with others on the team that is valuable and essential: new ideas and information emerge and the success of the organization is fostered.

Vision, Leadership, and Strategy – each critical to building your success.

As business owners, we are each committed to building and developing our businesses. Through intentional work and focus on the foundation, great success can be had. Focus on these critical foundational steps on the path to building great success. Refocus on them when your strategies drift off course. Always come back to the vision, your starting point and ending destination.

Chapter 20

W2 or 1099? The Wrong Choice Can Cost You Your Business

By James Hyland

You are running your business and you need to grow and hire help but you want to eliminate liability and minimize your headaches, so you tell your new hires that they will be 1099 independent contractors...smart idea, right? WRONG!

First, we need to address the correct definition of what is a true 1099 independent contractor. It is wholly your responsibility to determine if the person providing you service is a true independent contractor or an employee. The IRS will not give you any guidance except for some general definitions until after it is too late. The IRS will only give you guidance after the fact which can be determined through an IRS or state labor audit or a worker's compensation claim. A worker can complain that they were misclassified because they are seeking one of a few possible complaints against you or your company such as: that they want you to pay the employer side of taxes or, perhaps, seeking unemployment or disability benefits (an example is pregnancy) or worker's compensation benefits. Any of these or other possible aspects a worker can complain about to the state or the federal department of labor can result in fines and penalties for misclassification and potential tax liability exposure. An example of the tax liability is being held responsible for the taxes you did not collect from the employee and the employee's portion of the taxes if they failed to pay them because you, as a company, are a government-appointed collection agent. Also, penalties on any and all taxes on the aforementioned because your payments are now late. Also, fines can be levied for misclassification of a worker's status. The end result of paying in cash is the same as when you misclassify an independent contractor which includes the fines and penalties, etc.

IRS Definitions:

1099 Independent Contractor

A person operating their own business or trade that offers their services to the public or other companies. The determining factors of what makes a sub-contractor is defined by the varying levels of control. There are three common rules which all must be met:

1) Who is in control of the work and the worker? Aspects such as: time tables and controlling the standard of how the work is completed. Other aspects may include: where to purchase materials and who to hire, as in sub-contractors; where and when to purchase supplies for the job as in quality of supplies and materials.

2) Who is in control of the financial aspects? Such as: time tables for payment; who sets the rate payment; and whose tools and supplies are being used. For true contractors there must be opportunities for profit and loss.

3) Type of relationship? Aspects such as the contractor's business must exist without this job. They must have other opportunities; they must invoice (on letterhead with their company address and phone number) for their work; they must have a business card and business phone number; and they must have a contract stating how this work was paid for under the contractor's terms. Contractors are paid by contracted hourly rate or by the job where employees are paid weekly or hourly. If there is a permanency to the work on a full time basis, then that is going into and under the category of a W2 employee. The contractor must prove that he has the available time to work for others.

W2 Employee

There are 3 types of employees:

1) Someone who works under your control and direction in your work environment. How many days worked and how many hours per day worked as well as compensation are all established by the business owner.

2) A Statutory Employee is basically someone who could qualify as an independent contractor under the first set of employee rules but may be treated as an employee for tax purposes. They must meet certain conditions that all the work is to be primarily performed by them personally and they do not have a substantial investment in tools used to perform the tasks. The services are performed on a continuous basis on a year-round basis.

3) A Statutory Non-Employee. Only works for the one company but the employee controls their own hours and services are performed under contract. This is most common in sales organizations such as real estate sales where the broker tells the agent that the agent cannot work for any other agency but the agent can dictate most of their own work details.

In summary, if you have a temporary need, the most intelligent course of action is to utilize the services of a temporary employment agency which removes the burden from you, the business owner, as to the classification of the worker and the liability for filing taxes for the employee as well as any potential future unemployment and disability claims as well. If your needs are more long term, protect your business and tread very carefully.

Chapter 21

Should I Hire An Intern?

By Michele J. Alexander, B.A., CP

Whenever I have had the good fortune to have interns working in my company I have also had the good fortune of maximizing this work experience in ways that truly benefitted the interns as well as accomplished goals and objectives not attained for reasons you probably already know: not enough hours in the day; not enough days in the week; not enough weeks in the month or months in the year; poor cash flow; and already overworked staff. When used properly, internships can actually help your business to grow in many ways.

My first exposure to having interns was not really a good one since it was not my choice to have one; nor my decision. Nor was the person astute enough to handle the day-to-day grind and fast pace of the daily business operation since the owner of this business placed this person in a position that paralleled mine. It was, however, the one experience that helped me to understand how to maximize efficiency of a business intern if I were ever to have the opportunity of having an intern work directly for me. That experience taught me what to do and what not to do to make the intern experience work on all levels for my business and for the intern.

The only way to make interning work is to follow three simple rules:

1. Never allow your intern to work on daily routine tasks;

2. Never allow your intern to work longer than the task requires; and

3. Never allow your intern to be the first point of contact for your company.

Since your company is already in operation, don't stop the momentum of your daily operation by putting your intern in the middle of an already successful work day. It's not necessary and it will only serve to create a re-invented wheel....big mistake. Instead, before hiring your intern, take inventory on those projects that have not gotten off the page or out of the file cabinet or placed in your daily operation. Those projects, as you already know, are the ones that would amplify your daily operation since they were designed to be part of the company expansion you have been trying to put into motion and have not been able to do so. An expansion that amplifies and grows the business, interrupts, encumbers, or interferes with the basic operation.

Internships are not only a necessity but an irreplaceable piece of the learning experience for those involved. From a business perspective, interns provide innovative and fresh ideas and, in return, the intern receives an invaluable experience that only comes about in a workplace setting. When you hire an intern, you are placing you and the intern in a position to make a great mark on you, themselves, the workplace, and the very special project you have assigned for them to complete which can and will certainly elevate your company's level of production which naturally translates into increased profits and accomplishes the expansion, without interruption, of your customary, normal daily routines.

The intern experience can be all knowing, all powerful, and certainly all meaningful. As the intern's work starts to take shape, he/she gains the ability to apply theories and concepts learned in the classroom to real working situations because you are providing them with valuable field experience that is more than suitable for entering this very competitive job market as an entry level professional. Any and every assigned task you give an intern should also align them with opportunities to network with professionals in their given field since many colleges require internships as substantial to complete as part of one's coursework.

I have had interns working on expansion projects for the past four years and, as a result of their work products, I have been able to expand my operation to include facets of services that would have otherwise cost me thousands of dollars to implement. I operate two separate businesses one of which was stagnate and not gaining any momentum simply because I could not keep up with the changing technology needed to make and keep that business competitive. I had the projects and knew exactly what was needed to be done but not the financial resources in order to make it happen. Four years ago, when I received a call, a cold call, from an organization counselor looking for intern opportunities for her client caseload, I decided that perhaps this was a way to get the help I needed without it costing me an arm and a leg.

The counselor sent me the resumes of four young people all of whom were college freshmen. She said I could choose any one of them. However, when I looked at each of their profiles, I immediately saw the benefit of having all four of them since each one of them had a specialty that would benefit all of the expansion projects I needed achieved in order to give my business that competitive edge. So, I hired all four in the intern capacity.

Those interns gained experience in project management, accounting, legal work, non-profit management, event planning, and general office applications. I created several projects and provided each one the opportunity to be the lead on one project from start to finish. This included meeting deadlines, sitting in on meetings, reaching out to other professionals, and performing research. They even created additional websites, provided me with social networking connections which gave us visibility in the marketplace I did not have, created a media forum for us to be seen on YouTube, and established themselves as liaison connections which impacted and closed the generation gap giving my business a new generation of consumers. It gave them a sense of belonging, ownership, and responsibility that not only enhanced their educational mandate but also totally prepared them to enter the workforce as a truly experienced entry level professional.

Chapter 22

Background Investigations

By Eric B. Segal

In order for an entrepreneur to grow and not just survive in today's economy, he or she must balance a strong Offense with a supporting Defense which will compliment his or her talents and weaknesses.

The easiest and cheapest way to filter out undesirable candidates is to simply inform all candidates that a thorough background investigation is standard operating procedure and that all candidates should be honest and up-front. You may further state at your option that having any skeletons in the closet will not necessarily preclude an individual's candidacy; however, dishonesty or a lack of disclosure will.

As a general rule, never state words to the affect that: "You will get an offer after passing a background investigation" as this could put the employer in a potentially precarious legal position. A better phrasing might be to state that: "We make our decisions AFTER receiving the result of a thorough background investigation".

When considering whether or not a background investigation is a worthwhile pursuit, consider the following facts:

Between one-quarter to one-third of background investigations will yield at least one fact to merit a company to conclude whether or not an individual is truly the right candidate or partner for the position or role.

A bad business decision will usually cost you more than a good business decision will make you. Many bad decisions will put an organization out of business entirely. The author of this book is reminded of a close friend that lost their growing multi-million dollar business due to the lack of a simple non-compete agreement for its employees to sign; a bad business decision that cost the business owner everything.

Another gold nugget is to be sure to select the right advisors. This holds true both personally and professionally and is in alignment with another piece of wisdom that holds that you are judged by the company you keep. In life, the right personal and professional advisors will enhance you. The same may be said going in the opposite direction; the wrong advisors can and will destroy you. Using the above logic, one may ask if using a neutral advisor is even worth your time or effort? Would you go to a "fair-weathered friend" to ask for potentially life-altering advice? Using similar logic, what good is a professional advisor that will simply nod their head in agreement with your every thought? You would be better served trading this advisor in for a massage therapist; it would be cheaper and you would feel better at the end of the session. In contrast, a knowledgeable and argumentative advisor is someone that will continually challenge your ideas and add arrows to your quiver, so to speak.

Suppliers and vendors are another important aspect of your business. These are also your business partners that will bring your business to a grinding halt in the event that the relationship sours. Your vendors should be reputable, financially stable, and have the ability to deliver on their Service Level Agreements (SLA's). Performing a background investigation on your vendors is both prudent and responsible and will demonstrate to your customers and your vendors that you are serious about your business, your customers, and the overall success for all parties involved.

Your customers – Are you so desperate as to take on any customer only to be stiffed on the bill when it comes time to collect? Performing a background investigation on potential customers will have the double benefit of showing your customers that you are serious while also protecting your bottom line.

Your business requires an affordable and effective business defense. Simply informing an interested party that you will perform a background investigation on them will have the effect of weeding out undesirables. Remember: The good relationships will not be offended; the bad ones have something to hide.

Below are some of the excuses I have heard for why a business owner does not protect their bottom line by knowing the parties that they are employing or transacting business with.

"It costs too much!"

"I am a great judge of people"

"You just can't get honest references"

"I don't have the time to do this"

"I don't have the money"

If any of the above excuses sound like you then you are setting yourself up for failure. I will conclude this chapter with real-life outcomes for background investigations that were performed. You may judge the potential outcome.

- Someone was to invest $2M into a business. That investor wanted to research the current owners and research showed that one of the principles was sued by the FCC for violation of SEC laws.
- Investigations normally go back 7 years – One person was convicted of stalking 13 years ago and the business owner wanted to decline employment on other grounds and further investigation found that the applicant had forged their college transcript – not even sure if the applicant attended but never graduated as verified with college.

- Small company was hiring a Chief Financial Officer and the company performed an investigation and the applicant had falsified their college degree and when confronted the applicant admitted that she did it because "no one ever checks".

- A nanny who was working for a friend of the family wanted to do a verification check and came to find out that the nanny was driving the children of the friend's family on a suspended driver's license.

- A Board of Education wanted to check on a potential school bus driver. The applicant was driving on a suspended driver's license. A camp's counsellor drove a car into a truck and killed several children. It turned out that the license was provided but they were driving on a suspended license while driving 115 miles per hour.

- Over a 2-year period over 12 applicants applying for a teaching position at a specific college were found to have lied about even attending the college listed on their resumes and even presented forged transcripts.

I have done a lot of work with medical facilities and found that this is an especially needed area (due to high premiums of medical liability and malpractice insurance) since abnormally high incidences of negative outcomes of background investigations.

Chapter 23

18 Questions To Your Next Right Hire

By Joanne Lucas

Employers are taking longer to make decisions on who to hire for their opportunities.

There are many reasons for this. Fear of making the wrong decision is the prevalent reason. Often, the thought is "that if this person is excellent, there must be someone even better" which delays the hiring process. Meanwhile, the job is not getting done. With proper preparation, a decision can be made quickly and accurately.

Before interviewing, please ask yourself the following questions:

1. What are the job duties that need to be accomplished?
2. Who has done the best job so far?
3. What would you change in past employees to make the next employee for this position more efficient?
4. What have you liked in experience from the employees that have worked for you?
5. How much money are you losing due to not having an employee in this position?
6. What was the background of excellent employees that best fit your company's culture?

You also need to assess the following in order to make the right hire for your open position, department, and company:

1. Are you willing to train?
2. Are language skills necessary?
3. What computer skills are needed to be able to be an effective employee?
4. What are your goals for this opportunity?
5. Are you looking for someone who comes in, does the job, and goes home?
6. Are you looking for someone with creativity who can make recommendations?
7. Are you looking for someone who can be promoted to your position?

Three people may have the same qualifications yet their goals may be different from yours. Your assignment is to find the person with the skills who has the same goals as you do.

Is your salary and benefit package commensurate with other opportunities in your field and geographical area? If you pay too little, you may hire someone who needs a job but will leave when something more in their salary range comes up.

There are different ways to reward employees. Most employees do not leave for salary alone. The following questions will help you understand if you have the work environment that keeps good employees from leaving:

1. Are your employees praised for good work or ideas?
2. Is your company known for allowing a great quality of life (while still accomplishing goals)?
3. When candidates come in for interviews are they welcomed?
4. Do they see smiling employees?
5. Does your organization have a reputation for treating its employees well?

If not, you will only hire people who are desperate and who will leave as quickly as possible.

Is there training in either software or new trends in your field of work?

I once heard a conversation between two hiring authorities. One said that the employees wanted to go to school and that he was afraid that if he/she sent the employees to training that they would leave. His associate said that he/she would be more concerned that if the employee had no training that he/she would stay.

Have you discussed the qualifications with all you will be interviewing? If not, excellent candidates may be missed without knowing the reason why.

A wise man once said that you cannot know when you find something unless you know what you're looking for. Unless you and everyone on your team is on the same page as to what is needed, mistakes can be made.

As to the questions to ask, many employers are concerned about asking "illegal questions". In my experience, all the "illegal questions" go back to one: "Will you be here to do the work?" If you have any questions as to which questions are not appropriate, each state has its own laws but remember that by asking questions that may insult the candidate and you may miss out on a great employee.

Ask questions that need more than a yes or no. What are your favorite accomplishments? What problems have you had and what have you done to overcome them?

What do you know about our company and our line of work? What excites you about the opportunity? Why are you looking to leave your present job? What are you looking for in a future employer and opportunity?

Ask about counter offers. What will it take for your current employer to keep you?

Discuss salary and benefits if there is an interest on your part. By having an application, you will know what the person is currently earning. How does that compare with others who are doing a similar job? Be prepared to offer an increase for someone currently working, and a lateral for someone who isn't working.

If you're interested, set up a next step. If you're working with a recruiter, be sure to review the interview and how the person meets your legitimate requirements.

Be ready to make a decision if the candidate meets your skill and goal requirements.

Don't keep the mentality of "the grass is always greener, etc." Choose your next hire on their skills for your goal requirements as well as how well they fit into your culture and don't forget to use your gut instincts and of course, back ground investigations. Then, nurture them in your environment and you will be satisfied you made the right decision for the long term benefit for both your new hire and your company.

Chapter 24

Seven Techniques Employers Can Employ To Help Keep Employees Happy

By Brian T. Cody, CFP

Think to yourself: What would I want if I was an employee in my company? Then, try to figure a way to make it happen.

Get a 401(k) plan. It amazes me that only 14 percent of employers with fewer than 100 employees sponsor a retirement plan for their employees[1]. Sure, there are government regulations that must be followed and money that will come out of your business to help support the 401(k) plan, but how do you expect your employees to retire if you don't provide a system for them to save for the future?

Provide education. Use free online trading such as Khan Academy, Coursera.com, or search the Internet for a plethora of free online programs. Consider offering your employees a bonus when they complete certain programs within a specified time frame. You will have a more productive employee and that employee will appreciate their workplace.

Aim to grow your business by 5% or more per year. Common sense says that you need to grow your business if you want to have career advancement for your employees. Create a business plan that will allow you to grow your business and promote the best of your employees. I have heard many transitioning employees say "there was no place else to advance with my former employer so I had to leave".

Reward them with flexible hours. If you have employees that have a long commute, consider allowing them to drive to and from your office during off-peak travel hours. Or, if they worked primarily through the Internet, allow them work from home especially on the days before and after holidays. This type of perk is priceless.

Have fun in the office. If light music can improve the mood, play some music. If you can have a nice barbecue two or three times year, have a barbecue after work. I do suggest you keep the alcohol use to a minimum or, better yet, no alcohol; this is still a workplace.

Add a life insurance policy as a standard benefit for your employees. This is not always a large expense as an employer; however, it shows you are looking out for the families of your employees.

Use tools to ensure that you're paying your employees appropriately. Often, employees will complain that they are not being paid well. Have a benchmarking tool to show your employees that they are fairly compensated for their work. Use this tool during your annual employee review meeting to help your employees to understand that they are properly compensated.

1. Charles A. Jeszeck, "Retirement Security, Challenges and Prospects of Employees of Small Businesses," U.S. Government Accountability Office, July 16, 2013.

Chapter 25

Low to No-Cost Benefits to Attract and Retain Employees

By Katherine Woodfield Hermes

Thinking outside the box and opening your mind to employee life management issues is about more than just health insurance. Voluntary benefits, while not on a par with health coverage or retirement programs, are increasingly being added to employers' menus of employee benefits. Employers facilitate the availability of the benefits and employees individually choose and pay for those benefits that meet their needs in their lives. As long as employees are being asked to foot a portion of the bill, they should have some say in what they are paying for, right?

Voluntary benefits, also called worksite benefits, have been around for decades. They range from niche products such as pet insurance and identity-theft protection to coverage categories with wider appeal, such as automobile and homeowner's insurance. Employees' costs are often based on discounted group rates negotiated by the employer. The employer's expenses are typically limited to administrative costs, such as those for payroll deduction.

Some voluntary benefits are portable — meaning the employee can continue the coverage after leaving the company. Although some insurance benefits are sold as group policies, most are individual policies. The most popular benefits are still basic benefits — voluntary life and voluntary disability; however, there is a fast-growing category of benefits that consists of specialized medical coverage. Some types of coverage in that category are being expanded. For example, critical-illness insurance that once covered only cancer has been broadened in many instances to include heart attacks, major organ transplants, and other specific medical conditions or procedures. Typically, a lump-sum benefit of $10,000 to $50,000 is paid after a covered event occurs and the money can be spent on medical or non-medical needs.

When choosing a voluntary benefits provider, consultants suggest looking for vendors that have experience with voluntary benefits that have top financial ratings from A.M. Best or similar insurance rating agencies offer excellent customer service and administration. Like most things in life, you get what you pay for and the cheapest product isn't necessarily the best.

The secret to success is implementation and that means collaborating with vendors. The HR role is to quarterback the whole process meaning the HR person needs to have a handle on what's being done and who's doing it. Generally, HR sets up payroll deductions, facilitates communication with employees, monitors providers, and integrates providers' information with the employer's intranet. Included in this category are such items as life insurance, long-term care insurance, disability insurance, prepaid legal services, pet health insurance, and identity-theft protection. If an employee purchases automobile or homeowner's insurance through payroll deductions, rather than installments, the costs are automatically budgeted. Through some plans, employees can save $400 to $500 a year.

Some employers also subsidize voluntary benefits to sweeten the deal for participants. The gesture of generosity doesn't usually cost much as any benefit might have 30% to 40% employee participation and the costs are usually small as compared to the figures to which one is accustomed with respect to health care premiums.

The real question is "why not"? Voluntary insurance plans can resolve a bevy of market pressures faced by HR and benefits managers today at no cost to their companies. As a unique opportunity to satisfy competing priorities, voluntary insurance programs accomplish the seemingly impossible – to help create robust, affordable benefits packages in the face of diminishing budgets, rising healthcare costs, and a heated competition for talent.

Growing financial stress among employees can decrease morale, satisfaction, and productivity. Nearly one quarter of employers believe they are more likely to lose employees to competitors with better benefits packages. [1]

Employees feel that no other workplace benefit comes close in terms of importance. Among employers who currently or previously provided voluntary insurance,[2] the top reasons are to:

- Retain employees (23%)

- Increase job satisfaction (20%)

A company's benefit offerings affect its abilities to recruit and retain top talent.

Thinking Outside the Box About Health Insurance

The cost of health care continues to outpace inflation and household earnings at a pace greater than 2% to 11%. To reduce the burden on corporate bottom lines, benefit decision-makers are often forced to pass larger portions of these increases onto their workforce. The result, however, is that employees are now faced with some tough decisions with many resorting to drawing from personal savings, dipping into retirement accounts, and the increasing use of credit - all of which can lead to personal bankruptcy. When an employee faces financial difficulties an employer feels the impact as well in the form of decreased job performance, absenteeism, and dissatisfaction. At the same time, HR managers remain tasked with attracting and retaining the best employees.

For reasons I find very hard to fathom, many Americans have a difficult time taking responsibility for their own health care. We pay for things all day long but we don't want to pay to go to see the doctor.

We cut health care costs and improve our personal health care when we understand how health insurance is structured and change to the highly beneficial Consumer Directed Health Care (CDHC).

Re-orienting consumers is a difficult and uphill battle which cuts broker's commissions in half. Brokers can neither afford the time to explain this concept nor the loss of income that results from offering health insurance policies for half of the current rates.

Most health insurance consists of a "maintenance contract" and "catastrophe contract." Eliminate the maintenance contract and most Americans get healthier and save money.

<u>Analogy</u>: Home and auto owners pay for maintenance and insure against disaster. Following that successful structure, everyone who has a body should be responsible for general upkeep while being protected from disaster.

Insurance is designed to indemnify (protect) you and your assets. Out-of-control costs stem from looking to disaster indemnification providers to pay for our common low-risk or no-risk expenses.

In our current HMO/PPO/POS system, we pay for both "maintenance plan" and "catastrophe policy". The disaster part of the policy covers the lion's share of risk for the individual and yet significant consumer costs go towards the maintenance aspect of our policies.

Most people pay more in maintenance premiums then they claim in benefits (80% of Americans pay less than $700 per year in medical expenses). Why pay an additional $1,500 premium PLUS a co-pay so that the insurance will pay maintenance costs of $700 MINUS the co-pay?

Our current health insurance model is a two-part plan with a single premium that seamlessly, expensively, and unnecessarily provides both maintenance and disaster coverage. Most people do not realize that they can split apart those two components, save money, and better protect themselves and their families.

The solution is a High Deductible Health Plan (HDHP) or a Consumer Directed Health Plan (CDHP) linked to a Health Savings Account (HSA). Money we save in premiums (cash spent which we never see again) is instead invested into an HSA where cash accumulates, tax deductible, and tax free to pay future medical costs for ourselves and our families - the money is ours to keep.

Patients are empowered as costs drop as we comparison shop and negotiate routine bills. Doctors benefit as they are free to attend to patient health instead of insurance forms, multiple invoices, and collections. Insurance companies gladly pay for annual check-ups and preventative care, without deductible or co-pay, to incentivize people to stay healthy. The escalating cost of billing and claims processing dramatically decrease as we eliminate multiple layers of unnecessary middle men.

Most importantly and astonishingly (returning to our analogy just as people maintain their own cars and homes far better than the rentals they live in and drive), McKinsey & Co. statistics prove that with personal financial benefit, 25% of people make healthier choices.

The first step towards improving the current health insurance system is education – re-orienting every American towards taking responsibility for their body maintenance and towards health insurance as the indemnity plan for which it is designed. This becomes easy as we see the cash we are not wasting in premiums quickly accumulating in our own HSA bank accounts.

Other Benefits Your Employees Will Love

Employees of the sandwich generation have to balance the responsibility of their jobs, their families, and caring for a sick or elderly loved one. Hence, they are sandwiched between and often responsible for family members of both the previous and next generation. An estimated $33 billion is lost due to turn over, replacement, stress, lost productivity, and care-giving related absences. However, employers can work with Patient Advocates to alleviate some of this stress and to improve productivity. For example, My Health Care Connect www.myhealthcareconnect.com). Employees who retain the services of Patient Advocates report better personal health and less stress than those who had no access to support. Employers who recognize these issues earn their employees' loyalty.

If you own a home, at some point it will need some attention. Broken furnaces, no heat, no water, and home repairs of all shapes and sizes take employees' minds off of their jobs. Being a resource for trusted contractors will be a tremendous relief for an employer. Every business is tough and home remodeling is no exception. The ability to recommend a contractor and leverage your firm's continued support is a valuable and free offering. We found BBJ Inc. Remodelers (www.bbjremodelers.com) in New Jersey. They strive for total customer satisfaction, have an amazing reputation, and are an awesome resource for your employees.

Another no-cost great benefit employers can offer their employees is help finding a used car. Car problems cause unexpected and unwelcome delays in work and productivity. A service that helps car buyers locate, test, and negotiate for high quality pre-owned cars that fit their budget can save both the employer and the employee from a potentially explosive situation. Auto hunters such as www.findpreownedcars.com can save time, stress, and money. With a network of 300 dealers nationwide, they can stress test the pre-owned vehicles and notify the buyer when a good deal has arrived that fits the request.

1. "Small Business 'Now More Than Ever,'" Aflac, Acceler-PULSE™, 2009.

2. "Market Structure: Decision-Makers," TNS Taylor Nelson Sofres, 2006.

Chapter 26

Medical Care Discount Plans: An Affordable Alternative To Health Insurance

By Ciro J. Giue

The US Bureau of Labor Statistics estimates that 9.1% of the population in the US (or 14 million people) was unemployed at the end of August 2011. It is also estimated that 16.8% of all Americans (or 50.7 million) currently do not have any health insurance. In New Jersey, the figures are 9.4% of the population unemployed (or 421,676 people), and 12.6% (or just over 1 million people) uninsured. Unfortunately, given the poor state of the US and NJ economies, these figures may get worse before they get better. With the rising cost of health care and health care insurance many individuals and families are being forced to choose between going without health care and insurance coverage or putting food on the table. Even if the current health care reform package is enacted as written, many will still go without health care insurance and access to affordable care. Many do not realize that if health care insurance is not affordable to them and their families, they do not have to go without access to quality and affordable medical care for them and their families through a discount plan.

Let me begin by saying that in my opinion there is nothing better than health insurance to protect you and your family in the event of a medical condition. Whether it's a group plan through your employer or a non-group "individual" plan, health insurance typically provides the most robust coverage options for doctor office visits, hospital care, surgeries, medical testing, prescriptions, etc..... The challenge is that many employers are cutting benefits like group health insurance, requiring their employers to pay more of the cost of the premium, and sometimes cancelling group plans completely. Another challenge is that non-group individual health insurance plans in NJ are typically expensive, averaging well over $1,100 per month for the typical family plan. Medical Care Discount Plans enter today's landscape of high unemployment and large groups of uninsured to fill a void and provide access to affordable medical care where health insurance is not an option.

Medical Care Discount Plans in a Nut Shell:

- Provide an affordable alternative to insurance
- ARE NOT INSURANCE
- Participants pay a monthly fee for access to the discount
- Are designed for people who don't have insurance
- Provide a discount at the time the care is provided at participating care providers
- They accept everyone – No restrictions due to age or current/past medical conditions

Sample of Medical Care Benefits These Plans Provide:

- Doctor office visits, including specialists
- Ob/GYN Care
- Prescription Medications
- Radiology
- Hearing Testing
- Dental Care (incl. stand-alone dental plans)
- Vision Care (incl. stand-alone vision plans)
- Chiropractor
- Labs and Diagnostics
- Patient Advocacy

The monthly fee for these plans varies with the level of benefits they offer and usually runs between $19.95 - $79.95 for a single and $29.95 - $120.00 for a family. Specific Coverage Plans are also available for things like Dental and Vision care at cheaper rates ranging from $8/month single and $14/month family.

Discount plans are NOT INSURANCE, so they are not regulated like insurance plans, so buyer beware.

Questions you should ask before you enroll in any Medical Care Discount Plans:

- Is there an application fee?
- Are the fees guaranteed for 1 year or will they change?
- What are the benefits offered?
- Can I see the discounted fee schedule?
- Are there limits to how many times the plan can be used in 1 year?
- Are my current medications covered?
- Are there any monthly administration costs?
- How do I cancel the plan?
- What Care Providers are in your network? (Confirm this with your doctors.)
- Are any care/conditions excluded?
- Whom do I call if I have questions?

These plans are easy to apply for. There is usually a simple, one-page application. They accept everyone regardless of age and/or medical condition. These plans do not have a waiting period and there are no claims/administrative forms; no referral is needed to see a specialist in the Network. So, if insurance is not an option because it is either not available or not affordable, Medical Care Discount Plans can provide an affordable alternative to access quality and affordable medical care.

Chapter 27

You Are Not Your Company

By S.E. Day

"A Corporation is an artificial entity operating on its own accord. It only needs you to manage its day-to-day operations."

You have taken the 'Leap of Faith' to start your own business. You have invested sweat, headaches, tears, fear, unpaid time, and money into your dream of operating your own business and being your own boss. You opened a bank account in your name 'doing business as' your company with your social security number. You have started your 2nd year of operation and your business has grown from an idea into a full operation out of your home office. You have built your customer base, branded your business, increased your sales, and started to show a profit in your business. Things are going well!

One day a customer contacts you to place a large order and you know you are on your way to achieving your desires. After checking your bank account(s), you realize you do not have enough cash flow in your business account(s) to fill the order for the customer. You know that once this order is filled and the transaction has been completed, you will have made a nice profit margin for your business. Then it hits you, "If I only had business credit, I could get this order completed without disrupting my cash flow." So the next day, you contact your vendor to inquire about opening an account. Your vendor wants to obtain your business credit profile before opening the account. You realize you do not have one. Your vendor cannot extend business credit to your business because you have no business credit. The best solution the vendor can offer is 50 percent down payment to get the order started and the remaining balance paid upon delivery, which will take 30 to 40 days to complete. The 50 percent down payment will wipe out your cash flow.

Shortly afterwards, you contact your bank to apply for a business line of credit. Your banker wants to obtain your personal and business credit reports, your business financial reports, and your business income taxes for the past two years. You realize you damaged or over extended your personal credit while building your business. You do not have a business credit profile. You do not have financial reports for your business, and you filed a net operating loss in your business for the past two years on your IRS tax form 1040. Your banker informs you the bank cannot open a line of credit for your business and your business is operating at a loss. Your banker also informs you the bank cannot open a personal line of credit because your personal credit in weak. In addition, you have 'maxed-out' your personal credit cards building your business so you are at a loss in trying to finance this transaction on your own.

You eventually go back to your customer to inquire if your customer can finance the transaction by providing cash up front but your customer informs you that his/her company provides a purchase order and only pays on delivery of goods. Now you have a decision to make: Do you over extend your cash flow and place your vendors, your employees, and your current personal creditors at risk of not being paid or do you inform the customer that you cannot fill the order?

This brief synopsis of a business situation is highly probable and many of you reading this can resonate with the passage and the decisions which come with it. Now, you may be creating several scenarios in your head as you read this passage to overcome the aforementioned obstacles to achieve your goal. That's the true entrepreneur in you! However, if you do not find a permanent solution to this problem, similar situations will happen again and again. Similar situations occur like this one every day and I am sure you can create a few of your own you have experienced.

Let's evaluate the scenario. This person did a few things wrong in the beginning, which led to this problem. Even though this person put a lot of time and energy into the startup phase of the business, the business was not properly structured with the corporate division office of the Secretary of State. Everything in the business was personally tied to the individual. The taxes (pass-through taxation), the bank accounts (doing business as or DBA), the personal credit were all closely tied to the business. Even though this business owner built the business from scratch, the business owner should not be the business!!

These facts are all too common in the business world. These facts are also RED flags for corporate creditors. First of all, this individual should NEVER operate his/her business under the banner of 'Doing Business As." It appears as if this business owner has something to hide about the business operations. To add, the business owner is personally tied to the debts and liabilities of the business. This decision screams a red flag to corporate creditors. It does not show legitimacy for a corporate creditor. Because this business owner is operating as a Sole Proprietor, the owner has no legal protection from the misfortunes of the business. If this owner is sued by a vendor or customer for breach of contract or failure to deliver; or a customer falls at the business owner's residence while receiving a package; or the business owner is involved in an accident while delivering products; or a number of other varied scenarios, the customer, vendor, State, or IRS can attach the business owner's personal assets to the lawsuit and completely decimate this owner's personal finances. The business owner could not only lose his/her business but also his/her home, car(s), and personal savings as well.

Second, this business owner opened an account at the bank in his/her name 'doing business as' the company while using his/her social security number. Once again, this owner is personally tied to the business finances. There is no separation of personal and business finances. This can be seen by the Internal Revenue Service (IRS) as commingling of finances. This procedure also has broader implications because the IRS will also view the business owner as self-employed for tax purposes. This business owner can be assessed significant fees and penalties for Self-Employment Tax when filing his/her individual taxes.

Third, the business owner is personally liable for all of the business debts. If the business fails, the business owner's personal credit can suffer. The loss of income will put the business owner's livelihood in jeopardy. In most situations similar to this one, the business owner has had to file for Chapter 7 bankruptcy or federal court protection from creditors after being sued by a customer because of a major slowdown in business operations.

This example happens to be one of many scenarios business owners face every day of operating their businesses. In my years of being a business consultant, I have seen many cases of Sole Proprietorship which have gone in disarray because the business owner failed to structure their business properly.

When business owners properly structure or corporate their businesses within their state of residency as well as with the IRS, business owners take the first step in making their businesses attractive to corporate creditors. According to the IRS, there are five recognized business structures starting with 1) Sole Proprietorship; 2) Limited Liability Company; 3) Partnership; 4) S-Corporation; and 5) General Corporation or C-Corporation. Again for IRS purposes, your form of business structure will determine the particular income tax you will have to file. **Please understand acquiring your tax identification number (TIN) or employer identification number (EIN) from the IRS is the second step and not the first step.** A number of business owners are operating their businesses with only their TIN/EIN. Before an entrepreneur applies for a TIN/EIN from the IRS, the entrepreneur should choose the appropriate business structure, complete the appropriate paperwork in order to legally structure the business, and submit the paperwork and fees to the state.

Over the years, I have attempted to conduct business with business owners who only had their TIN/EIN while claiming their businesses had a particular business structure. After researching their companies, I had to contact those business owners and inform them that my company could not conduct business with their companies because they had not structured their companies properly.

This brings me to the first step of operating a successful business and making your business corporate credit ready. I previously mentioned the different levels of corporate structure as recognized by the IRS. I am going to delve deeper into the structures, what they mean, and which ones are best to attract corporate creditors.

The first business entity is the **Sole Proprietorship (SP)**. The SP is the simplest form of business structure. The SP does not have a legal representation in most states. The SP statute is granted to an unincorporated business owned by an individual. Under the SP statute, the business owner and the business are one in the same. The business owner is entitled to all of the profits of the business and responsible for all of the liabilities and losses. The business owner is viewed as self-employed by corporate creditors as well as the Internal Revenue Service. This is not a good position to be in for a number of reasons already explained but more importantly for the sake of this chapter. Under this business structure, the business owner cannot master the business credit maze. Corporate creditors do not consider this type of business structure to be a business.

I am sure many of you reading this statement will disagree because you may be carrying a credit card with your business name affixed to it in your handbag or wallet. While that may be true, the credit card in this case is actually attached to you personally. It was granted because you have an account with your bank and the bank used your personal credit history to offer the card. This type of practice by your bank creates a false sense of business credit and can actually do more harm than good to your personal credit.

When a bank does this, you as a business owner believe you are establishing credit for your business. You will, in turn, continue to seek other credit from other creditors. Each time, the creditors will use your personal credit score and history to offer you credit. This dangerous practice can and will put you and your business in financial jeopardy.

The second business entity is the **Limited Liability Company**. The Limited Liability Company or LLC is a relatively new term in the world of business. The concept of limited liability companies originated in Wyoming in the late 1970s. This concept has been evolving ever since its inception. Until 1996 and the creation of the Uniformed Limited Liability Company Act (ULLCA), each state had drafted some form of legislation to address the limited liability company. Even after the 1996 creation of the Act, only nine states had adopted the ULLCA by 2006. Before the creation of the LLC, business owners only had a few choices of corporate structuring which involved many rules and regulations for the business owners to adhere. Full liability protection was afforded to only shareholders of corporations.

The Limited Liability Company structure was instigated out of a desire to have a form of legal liability protection while maintaining the status as a 'pass through' entity afforded to partnerships. As defined by the IRS, a 'pass-through' entity passes its income, loss, deductions, or credits to its owners. The owners may be partners, shareholders, beneficiaries, or investors. It usually does not have an entity level income tax liability. The pass-through policy is a benefit because the IRS affords the business owners of certain business entities the benefit of carrying a business entity's profits and losses on the individual business owner's personal tax filings.

With an LLC, the members and/or managers receive the benefit of liability protection and are taxed by the IRS at their individual tax rate because the LLC itself does not pay federal income tax. This 'pass-through' taxation gave many states the incentive to receive more taxes from the number of members an LLC could have. Also, with LLCs in most states, the members and/or managers are not required to be listed on the LLC's articles of organization or certificate filed with the Secretary of State corporate division office.

According to the *National Conference Commission on Uniform State Laws*, "a limited liability company has members who primarily contribute capital to the company and who share in the profits or losses. It may have managers who do the business of the company. A member may be a manager, but non-member managers are also allowed. A limited liability company statute has certain key features: a means of creating the company, usually by filing a certificate; a liability shield provision; rules governing the relations between members, and between members and any managers; rules governing distributions of profits or losses to members and a member's creditor's rights; rules governing a member's exit rights from the company; rules on dissolution of the company; and rules governing mergers and conversions. A limited liability company is usually governed by an operating agreement that almost always supersedes and overcomes the statutory rules." Members or managers of an LLC can be single-members, corporations, or other LLCs. Members and managers could leave the LLC without any personal liability for the company's actions. This maneuver by members or managers is the key reason corporate creditors are leery of providing business credit to limited liability companies.

The LLC has become a desired business entity because it allows the members and/or managers to tailor the company to a specific objective as long as it is agreed upon by the members and/or managers. This was a great concept because it expanded the many uses of business and opened doors for many businesses to be created. The Internal Revenue Service's website states, "Depending on elections made by the LLC and the number of members, the IRS will treat an LLC as either a corporation, partnership, or as part of the LLC's owner's tax return (a "disregarded entity"). Specifically, a domestic LLC with at least two members is classified as a partnership for federal income tax purposes unless it files Form 8832 and affirmatively elects to be treated as a corporation. An LLC with only one member is treated as an entity disregarded as separate from its owner for income tax purposes (but as a separate entity for purposes of employment tax and certain excise taxes), unless it files Form 8832 and affirmatively elects to be treated as a corporation."

Corporate creditors will want the LLC to have been in operation with the same leadership for a period of three years or more before extending business credit. Many corporate creditors will also require the members and/or managers of the LLC to personally guarantee any credit or loans the LLC receives. The drawback with an LLC is that the concept allows the members and managers to be unseen or remain autonomous which creates a red flag for corporate creditors. With LLCs, the members and/or managers (business owners) are still directly connected to the company for credit purposes.

I have advised business owners who have followed this practice for years believing they were building business credit for their companies. Suddenly, the business owners default on the payments or become overextended and their entire credit profiles begin to shift and suffer as a result.

The following is one of a few Case-In-Points to be used to illustrate examples of ways to destroy business credit and of ways to build business credit.

Case-In-Point (1):
I consulted with a business owner who had successfully built a business in the travel industry for more than 10 years. The business owner's personal credit score was over 780 points and this business owner had amassed more than $600,000 in credit limits from several major credit cards providers. The business owner had the capacity to purchase anything for the business or for home. The business owner decided to purchase a high-end luxury vehicle. After two months of ownership, the business owner decided that it was not the right vehicle and decided to return it. The business owner contacted the dealership and advised of the decision to return the car. The business owner further advised the dealer to come and get the vehicle. The dealership did not respond in the manner the

business owner desired so the business owner decided to stop paying for the vehicle.

Several months passed and finally the finance company contacted the business owner about the lack of payment. The business owner advised the finance company of the conversation with the dealership and the desire to return the vehicle. The business owner was advised by the finance company this action would be reported on the business owner's credit report as a voluntary repossession and the business owner's credit score would be personally affected.

Eventually, the business owner's credit score was affected as advised by the finance company and the business owner's credit score dropped to the low 600s. This action caused a 'domino' effect and several of the credit card providers reduced the business owner's credit limits by a minimum of $100,000 per card. Because the business owner's personal credit was tied to the pseudo-business credit, the business was being scrutinized by the creditors.

Had the banks advised this business owner of the apparent risks of being personally connected to the business credit of the company, the business owner could have avoided the company's credit being scrutinized by the banks. Also, this business owner was not operating as a sole proprietorship. This business owner's company was actually structured as a single-member Limited Liability Company (LLC) but the business owner had not elected the LLC to be treated as a corporation nor did the business owner treat the company like a corporation. The business owner's action and lack of knowledge caused the company's business credit to suffer.

The third business entity is the **Partnership**. The Partnership is a very old concept used in business. The partnership is the relationship created between two or more entities for a specific business purpose. For tax purposes, the IRS describes a partnership as the relationship created between two or more persons who join to carry on a trade or business. The IRS addresses persons because under the IRS rules, a corporation is considered an 'artificial' entity or person.

In addition, there are several different degrees of partnership which you must be aware of and these partnerships vary from state to state. Under general consensus, the partnerships are 1) General Partnership (GP); 2) Limited Partnership (LP); 3) Limited Liability Partnership (LLP) or Professional Limited Liability Partnership

(PLLP); and 4) Limited Liability Limited Partnership (LLLP).

1. **General partnerships** are composed of two or more persons who agree to share in on the profits, losses, liabilities, and assets of a business venture. This entity usually does not require a formal structure with the secretary of state. The formal terms are normally contained in a written partnership agreement.
2. **Limited partnerships** are generally made up of one or more general partners and one or more limited partners. The general partners manage the business and share fully on the profits and losses while the limited partners share in on the profits of the business. Limited partners' losses are usually limited to the amount of their investment.
3. **Limited Liability** or **Professional Limited Liability partnerships** are similar to General partnerships except that one partner is not responsible for the liability or negligence of the other partners. LLPs and PLLP are usually business structures for lawyers or accountants.
4. **Limited Liability Limited partnerships** are limited liability partnerships which chose to include a statement designated them as such in the certificate of limited partnership. LLLPs are designed to protect the general partners from liabilities of the LLLP.

Each of the partnerships is designed for specific purposes. Regardless of the partnership, each person or entity contributes money, labor, skills, or property and is expected to participate in the profits or losses of the partnership. Each level of partnerships must be registered with the secretary of state except general partnerships. Remember, each state is different so check with a business attorney in your state before you consider entering a partnership.

Partnerships are similar to LLCs except the partnership must file an annual information report to the IRS to inform of the income, gains, deductions, losses, etc., from its operations, but does not pay income tax. Like an LLC, partnerships benefit from 'pass through' taxation of any profits or losses to its partners. Each partner will file its share of the partnership's income or losses on its tax return.

When it comes to corporate creditors offering business credit, partnerships are treated like sole proprietors. The corporate creditors will not base business credit on the partnership but on the individual partners instead. Each partner's personal credit profile will be used to establish credit for the individual partner and not for the partnership at all. Partnerships are not ideal for establishing business nor are they designed to receive business credit.

The next two business entities are the best business entities to establish and build business credit. Corporate creditors require <u>accountability</u> and <u>stability</u>. Corporate creditors want to do business with organizations that have written standards and procedures for conducting business operations. The Subchapter Corporation (S-Corp) and the General Corporation (C-Corp) provide the required accountability and stability needed by corporate creditors because state and federal regulators require more of these corporations. If you are starting a business and desire to build sustainable and long-term business credit, consider the following business entities.

The forth business entity is the **Subchapter Corporation**. The Subchapter Corporation or S-Corp is a general corporation with special tax election from the IRS. S-Corps are not automatically granted 'pass-through' taxation until the corporation qualifies for the status. In order to qualify to be an S-Corp, the corporation must meet certain requirements. The requirements are 1) Be a domestic corporation in the U.S.; 2) Not be an ineligible corporation i.e. financial or insurance institution; 3) Have no more than 100 allowable shareholders; 4) Have one class of stock. The one-class-of-stock rule thwarts the S-Corps from having the intricacies related to allocating earnings to multiple classes of owners. An S-Corp has only one class of stock if all outstanding shares provide for identical rights to stockholders regarding distribution and liquidation of proceeds. If an S-Corp issues a second class of stock, it ceases to meet the definition of a small business corporation, and its S-Corp status is automatically terminated. This termination will elicit significant adverse tax ramifications for its owners. However, differences in voting rights among shares of stock of a corporation do not automatically indicate that there is more than one class of stock. If your S-Corp meets the four requirements, then you have to file Form 2553—Election by Small Business Corporation with the IRS.

The S-Corp carries the same requirements as a corporation except for the 'pass through' entity taxation benefit. The restrictions are also minimized for S-Corps whereas the S-Corps must still have a board of directors but are only required to meet annually to record corporate minutes. The tax advantages are also better with an S-Corp than they are with LLCs, partnerships, or sole proprietorships. The fifth and by far the oldest and best business entity is the **General Corporation or C-Corp**. The corporation is as old as the country itself and it includes both profit and non-profit designations. Our forefathers fought for freedom of corporate control and taxation from Great Britain. As structured businesses started to emerge in the United States in the early 1800s, the government realized it could effectively collect business taxes under the Bureau of Internal Revenue (predecessor of the Internal Revenue Service). Corporations became the standard for taxing authorities, both state and federal, to collect taxes as a means of supplementing and enhancing the budget as well as to pay for the wars.

Corporations had to fulfill certain requirements before they could be recognized by the government. Corporations had to be registered with a governmental body and had to list their board of directors and corporate officers. Corporations also had to have and maintain locatable business addresses as would an individual. These requirements lead to corporations having a unique designation. Corporations are recognized as 'artificial entities'. In 1886, the Supreme Court made a determination in the case of Santa Clara County v. Southern Pacific Railroad recognizing corporations as holding the status of "corporate personhood". This determination was subsequently used as precedence to hold that a corporation was a 'natural person'. Through years of debating, corporations now carry the designation of 'artificial entity.'

The reason this designation is important in the world of business is because corporate creditors view corporation as corporate or natural persons. With this designation corporations became the standard when the issuance of business credit began to emerge as a viable means to conduct business without depleting a corporation's cash flow. Using the same standards and requirements as the government, the original corporate creditors i.e. banks and trust companies realized they could issue business credit to corporations because corporations had proven themselves to be accountable and stable.

The corporation must be registered within business owner's state of residency with the corporation division of the Secretary of State's office. The Articles of Incorporation are required to be filed for registration and they must list the board of directors as well as the president and/or chief executive officer. The corporation is required to have monthly board meetings with an annual board meeting for the election of it officers. The corporation is required to have shares of stock and the number of shares will be listed in the Articles of Incorporation. The corporation must have a legally and verifiable business address with a business telephone number. The state and IRS requires each corporation to have a tax identification number (TIN) and the number must be listed with the corporation division of the state. For federal tax purposes, the C-corporation is recognized by the IRS as a separate taxpaying entity. According to the IRS, the profit of a corporation is taxed to the corporation when earned, and then is taxed to the shareholders when distributed as dividends. <u>This creates a double tax</u>. The corporation does not get a tax deduction when it distributes dividends to shareholders. Shareholders cannot deduct any loss of the corporation. A corporation conducts business, realizes net income or loss, pays taxes and distributes profits to shareholders. A corporation is an independent legal entity. It is separate from the people who manage and own it or who share in its profits. In the tax laws, a corporation is viewed as a legal person who can enter into contracts, pay taxes separate from the owners, and incur debt. Since corporations are artificial entities, they will survive the business owners in the event of the business owner's death.

Understanding the historical power of corporations and the power corporations carry in today's society and economy, I finally understood the statement the gentleman told me, "The fastest way to wealth in America is to own a corporation." A corporation will allow you to do many more things you cannot do with a limited liability company or operating as a sole proprietor. It will also give your business tax advantages you cannot receive with a limited liability company, sole proprietorship, or S-Corporation.

Throughout this chapter, one thing should be apparent. <u>You are not your business</u>! In the best business practice, your business is your business and you should treat your business like a separate entity or person because it is. After many years of trial and error in owning the different types of business structure, I have come to realize each business structure serves a different purpose. As an entrepreneur or business owner, you must decide which business structure best suits your business needs. Choose the right business structure for your business idea or company and grow it accordingly. Corporate creditors, like any lenders of credit, are trying to minimize their risk in lending. They simply want accountability and structure to ensure they are not at a loss when providing your company business credit.

As a business finance advocate and consultant, I favor the business structures of S-Corps and C-Corps. I also favor them for credit building purposes. Corporations provide the accountability and stability needed to build a strong foundation to attract corporate creditors and other corporate vendors as well as investors. The tax advantages for corporations are more numerous than those of a limited liability company or partnership. Nevertheless, always consult with a business attorney and a business accountant in your state of residency to discuss which business structure would be best for your company.

An Important Note: If you have already established your company as a Limited Liability Company but desire to change it to a corporation, the process is simple. Contact the IRS and complete a new SS-4 requesting a change in status to a corporation. You will be allowed to keep your current TIN/EIN. You will also need to file Articles of Incorporation with the corporate division of your state and rescind your Articles of Organization for the Limited Liability Company. Remember to update your record with D&B Corporation as well. Everything must match in your corporate records.

Chapter 28

In-Person Business Networking

By Josh Dill

Have you ever heard the saying "People do business with people they like, know, and trust"? How about that the best way to get a new client is through a referral? Every business professional, sales person, and small business owner agrees that the above two beliefs are true. This being the case, it always surprises me that some small business owners and sales professionals are not aware of that attending professional networking groups and functions will increase their brand recognition and improve their sales. We also know that is it easier to increase sales through building long standing relationships which produce not only a steady stream of referrals but also amazing new relationships. When you build yourself a network of these valuable contacts in logical industries which are mutually beneficial to yours, that is known as "power partners" or "strategic alliances" and these individuals are most easily met at business networking events. As an example, an excellent pairing would be a real estate agent and a mortgage loan officer.

Yes, most people are aware of their local chamber but they are not aware how much more is available for business contact cultivation. You can build your client base via in-person networking in a variety of events during the month more aggressively than just belonging to the local chamber.

To make this strategy a successful part of your marketing plan you need 3 components. The first is your "elevator speech". Your "elevator speech" is a condensed way to explain to someone you meet what you do and who you would like to meet or who is your target prospect. Your elevator speech should be no more than 30 seconds and you should easily be able to memorize and, of course, make it interesting. The second is to understand the number one rule and successful strategy of all experienced networkers. This rule is best coined as a term from BNI, "Givers gain". In other words, always seek to help others and others will naturally want to help you in return. Nothing puts off networkers than someone who shoves a business card in their face while trying to pitch and close them on the spot.

The third is knowing where to go to attend networking meetings or events. The following are just a few examples.

- There are two extremely well known and successful national and international organizations you should consider: Le Tip and Business Network International (BNI).

- Professional organizations of your target market

- Networking groups for your religious affiliation – there is JBN – Jewish Business Network and, of course, you can Google one which best suits your needs.

- If you're a woman (men are welcome as affiliate members) please look at NAWBO – National Association of Women Business Owners – NAWBO has chapters per state and you do not need to be the owner of the business to attend or be a member. Sales people are welcome.

- Meetup.com – there are specialized chapters of meet up groups in all areas – take a look to see what makes sense for you.

- Having coffee with a contact from LinkedIn and asking them which networking events they are members of or frequent.

When attending networking events you need to keep in mind some "best practices". Some of these "best practices" include:

- Engaging people you meet to speak about themselves.

- Be an attentive listener. This helps your first impression be a good one.

- Ask a lot of questions – dig deep to get to know someone on a personal level without becoming intrusive. Practical tip - Remember to keep away from political or religious topics.

- When speaking about yourself, remember that this initial conversation which is meant to explain why someone would want to become a long term strategic partner with you. Do not speak in a sales pitching manner. This will only cause a person to glaze over and try to escape the conversation at their first opportunity.

- Remember, this is about quality – not quantity. It is better to meet only 3-5 people in a 2 hour event which you have had meaningful conversations with than scouting the room and quickly collecting 20 cards in that same 2 hours period.

After each networking event you should follow up within 1-2 days with who you met and suggest meeting over coffee or lunch to start building that long term mutually beneficial relationship.

Those who attend networking events are in the business of building long-lasting and mutually beneficial relationships which will hopefully lead to increased business for the ambitious sales executive or small business owner. Use the above tips and see how you can use in-person networking as one of your 5 tiers of marketing to grow your business.

Chapter 29

Public Speaking Skills For Business Owners and Sales Professionals

By Marlene J. Waldock

You are asked to give a presentation or maybe just introduce yourself at a meeting. All of a sudden your mouth gets dry, your breathing gets shallow, your palms start to sweat and when you stand up, your knees feel weak. You open your mouth to speak and it sounds like someone else's voice. Sometimes you are not even sure of what you said.

Sound familiar? Speaking in public is the most fear inducing act. Most people would rather die than give a speech or make a presentation. But as business owners and professionals in today's environment, you must be able to present your ideas and your business in a variety of venues - to promote your business

Even there are those who have a natural ability to be public speakers, it is something that you can learn. There are two major facets to good presentations - the message and the delivery

Consider this - a seasoned presenter can overcome a bad speech, a bad presenter can destroy a good speech and a novice presenter must start with a speech/presentation that is easy to deliver.

To put "pop" into your presentation you must:

- Prepare yourself
- Organize the material
- Present is as a conversation.

It's an easy process.

1. Begin with the core idea

2. Create a strong opening and closing

3. Have a conversation with the audience

What causes the most fear? That you will forget what you are supposed to say? That you will say something stupid? Or that you will stumble around trying to find the right words? You anticipate an outcome that is not going to happen.

First, no one in the audience expects you to be perfect. I am a 25-year veteran public speaker. I began my career in public speaking at an early age – doing how to pack your suitcase for a luggage manufacturer in my home town. I can tell you that the first time I gave the presentation I was petrified. I later went on to be a national training director for a fortune 100 company, where I presented a 4.5 Audio visual program - the first time I gave that presentation no one heard a word I said, and I had a microphone. I always tell my audiences that if I say something that they didn't understand, or if I say something that makes no sense – to please stop me. I tell them from the beginning that I am not perfect.

Secondly, when you follow this process your presentation will be very easy to deliver.

1. Begin with the core idea

Prepare yourself. What is your message? Keep it simple!

Ask yourself these questions: Why am I there, why is the audience there? What outcome am I seeking?

What outcome are they seeking? Then you must consider the following: Time of day, other activities, is this an open presentation or mandatory, are they paying or is it free?

Your preparation is all about the audience. Your goal is to make them comfortable because:

~ They want you to be successful.

~ They want to learn something from you.

~ And they don't care if you are perfect.

2.   Create a strong opening and closing

First impressions count - capture the audience's attention - create an interesting/strong opening. Set the stage - why are you giving your presentation. What is the expected outcome – make it clear.

Rule of the 7's - 7 seconds to make an impression – 7 seconds to capture attention – 7 seconds to tell your story in introduction summary. If you lose the audience in the first few seconds, they won't pay attention to what you are trying to say.

There are a variety of openings from asking a question to making a profound statement and taping into the audiences emotions to stating a fact.

The audience is there to learn something - let them know that what you have to say is something of interest.

Closing - first and last out rule - create a strong closing – leave them with something to think about.

3.   Have a conversation with the audience

How you do you do that? Envision yourself talking to a friend. Have eye contact with everyone in the audience as though you are talking to them. When you focus on the audience you can't think about yourself. The presentation becomes passionate, informative, and real.

Tell stories and paint a verbal picture. Speak from the heart and talk about that which you know well. To accomplish your goal, you need only to have one to three points.

Before you close – ask for questions. Never, and I mean never, close your presentation on a question from the audience. You want to have the last word.

Present - don't encumber yourself with a lot of Powerpoint slides. In fact, unless you have some unbelievable pictures to support your points, don't use Powerpoint at all. There is nothing worse than a slide with a bunch of words on it. They came to hear you speak not to read what you have to say.

This is all about you. It's time to "pop.

Chapter 30

Practical Marketing for Every Business Budget

By Ronald Hatcher

What line item is usually among the first to be cut from the budget when business is slow? You probably surmised that it is advertising and other forms of marketing a company's products or services. There are times when this is an absolute necessity but keep this in mind: Marketing and advertising are the lifeblood of any business. Study upon study has shown that businesses that cut back marketing budgets significantly suffer greater business slumps than those businesses that reduce spending slightly or don't cut the budget at all.

If working with a small budget is unavoidable, it doesn't mean that you should throw up your hands and say "I give up" and just put the money in your pocket? Absolutely not! Advertising is not really an expense. It is an investment. You do not stop investing simply because you have less money to invest. If you are a smart investor, you seek out investment advice and you also seek low-cost investments that still offer a good rate of return. Apply this same principle to advertising and you can reap big rewards from small expenditures.

Below is a list of things you can do to market your business without breaking the bank. It is not all-inclusive but illustrates the diversity of approaches. Some of these you can do yourself while others should be handled by a marketing professional. Enlisting the help of a professional is often less expensive than you think. In fact, if you are buying media such as TV, Radio, Print, Outdoor, or certain forms of Online, the media professional is paid a commission by the media thereby making the professional's services to you free.

1. Television – You don't have to buy a spot on The Super Bowl for $3 million to make a splash. Local Cable TV is more affordable than many business owners think. You can keep your costs down by buying only one cable system within your business' core geography. Most important of all, producing the commercial can cost as little as $2,000. Better yet, it may be produced for free by the cable system that your TV commercial will run on. In other words, if you purchase a schedule from the cable operator, they may produce your commercial for free.

   Another means of reducing costs is to purchase a "DR" schedule. DR (direct response) rates are lower, however the cable operator reserves the right to not run any spots that comprise your DR schedule if they can be sold for higher, "regular advertiser" rates. The nuances of planning and negotiating a TV schedule are such that you may want to enlist a professional's assistance because they can usually save you money and save you a few headaches along the way.

2. Radio – Here's a little secret: You do not need to buy a lot of radio spots for a successful campaign. On more than one occasion, I have seen a single radio commercial generate telephone calls and website visits. By the way, these were not award-winning commercials. They were simple and to the point, but they struck a chord with the listeners and left them with a way to get in touch with the business. The last point is the most important point. Make sure the commercial says the phone number and/or web address a minimum of two times. If possible, three times is better.

   If you can't afford to hire a copywriter to do a script for you, it is okay. Write the first draft yourself. You can submit this to the radio station(s) and they will usually edit it and record it for free.

   Radio advertising costs vary greatly depending on the size of the market, the size of the audience listening to the station, the time of year and the time of day that the commercial will run and the actual supply of available commercial time that the station has to sell. A spot in a market such as New York or Los Angeles will cost much more than a spot in Pueblo or Texarkana (TV costs vary for the same reasons).

Radio schedules costing as little as $1,000 have proven to be effective in big markets such as New York. So, depending upon where your business is based, you can scale it down accordingly.

3. Print – The Internet has hurt Print more than any other media category. This spells opportunity for savvy entrepreneurs. Publishers are more accommodating than ever before. The costs for advertising in newspapers and magazines are highly negotiable. The most important thing to keep in mind is that larger size ads will usually garner more readership, but generally speaking, the law of diminishing returns is in effect. What this means, for instance, is that a full-page ad will usually not deliver double the sales of a half page ad nor will a half page deliver twice as many sales as a quarter page. Most studies suggest that there is better return-on-investment (ROI) in smaller ad sizes relative to larger sizes.

In order to keep your costs down, design an attractive ad but one that limits itself to the most vital information and can be relatively small. It's better to run two small ads than one large one. Message frequency will help your customers remember you. You will also reach a slightly larger audience because not everyone reads every issue of a publication.

There are some publications that will actually run advertising on a pay-per-lead basis. The marketer only pays the publisher for legitimate leads. This is not a common practice, but it's worth exploring, since it can result in tremendous savings.

Community newspapers and other weekly and bi-weekly publications, such as The PennySaver also deliver great results for many marketers without requiring huge outlays. If you see one of your competitors running in the PennySaver virtually every week, that's a sure sign that it is worth testing. A half page, full color ad with a circulation of 50,000 can be purchased for around $500. Again, negotiation is the order of the day. If you don't have the time to haggle, get a professional to do it for you. You will save money and recapture the time you need to run your business.

Ads in school yearbooks are very inexpensive and subject to repeat exposure over several years.

4. Direct Mail – As many of you know, doing a direct mail campaign for your individual company can be expensive. Interestingly, though, it remains a staple for so many small businesses because it still works and in many cases delivers one of the best ROI's available. There are ways to keep your costs down and still get the benefits that direct mail offer. If your product or service lends itself to be among other marketer's offerings, consider one of the cooperative or group mailing products available, such as ValPak. ValPak's famous blue envelope has come to represent savings for most Americans. If you want to "jump-start" your sales consider a coupon or some type of promotion that will drive response. You can reach about 50,000 homes for $1,000 to $2,000.

Welcome Wagon is a direct marketing program that targets new homeowners. About 16% of Americans move each year. Of the 16%, nearly half move to a different county. Welcome Wagon offers a few low-cost solutions to target the newest arrivals in your neighborhood.

5. Out-of-home / Outdoor – Anyone who has ever investigated the cost of a billboard (or bulletin as the largest units are referred to) knows that they can be very expensive. Some spectacular units in markets such as New York, Chicago and Los Angeles can cost upwards of $100,000 per month. However, this media category has seen tremendous growth, second only to that of the Internet. The increase in available options offers an opportunity for the astute marketer. Take a walk around your core business zone. Look for signage and other forms of out-of-home media that are not being utilized. The media company would rather make a little money selling a sign to you at a bargain rate, than leaving the media vehicle vacant or with an old, non-paying client reaping the rewards of free advertising.

Consider these other out-of-home options. Some of them include elements of events and print, but they won't cost you an arm and a leg:

- Sponsor an athletic event such as a 5K run. Typically, you will get a table, distribution of your business information in a "sponsor gift bag", and some signage.

- Create a flyer. Post it and distribute it wherever it is legally permitted. Posting in colleges, supermarkets, "mom and pop" storefronts, etc. can get the word out very inexpensively. Distribution of flyers can range from house-to-house to standing in a single high traffic location and handing them to passers-by. You can hire college students to help keep costs down or hire professionals who can guarantee a greater degree of success through various techniques they employ.

- Set up a table at the local fitness center/gym. Many establishments will allow you to rent some space at the front entrance where you can distribute literature, maybe include a special offer, and explain your unique selling proposition.

- Place advertising on your car. "Moving billboards" are well read and memorable. You do not have to turn your personal property into a "circus" to promote your business. Custom magnetic signs that you can easily mount and remove are the solution to advertising your business only when you want to. Again, follow the rule-of-thumb for outdoor signage: keep the message short. Provide the company name; state what the business does, if it is not implied in the name; list a telephone number and your company's website address.

- Rent a table/booth at local places of worship. Many churches, synagogues, etc. host various events and offer local businesses inexpensive sponsorship opportunities.

- Distribute balloons with your company's name, services, phone number and URL at events, charities, parties, parks, etc. Printing will typically cost between 5 and 20 cents per balloon depending on whether there is one-sided or two-sided messaging, size of balloon, and number/type of colors used.

- Distribute bookmarks with your company information. Of course, you must make sure your local library, bookstores, card shops, etc. will accept them and leave them in conspicuous places for consumers to happily take them home for free. You can put a substantial amount of information on bookmarks, so consider offering a discount, contest or promotion that drives people to call you or register on your website.

- Tee shirts, polo shirts, and baseball caps with printed or embroidered messages are all wonderful ways of staying in front of potential customers. These forms offer some of the least expensive means of "reminder" advertising available. A quality-printed tee shirt will last a long time. Not only does it remind the original recipient of the shirt, who and where he/she received the "gift" from, but it sends a message to others every time it is worn. Some of these items are so cherished that they outlive the companies whose products and services they promote.

- College campuses can be a very attractive venue, if your product lends itself to teens and young adults. Check to see if universities in the area allow vendors to set-up tables at events. You may be allowed to post a small sign in the student union building or cafeteria. Leaflets may also be permitted. There are also professional companies that can recommend various types of college-oriented media to you.

- Medical practices may offer inexpensive media opportunities. Perhaps you know a doctor who does not offer enough reading material in the waiting room. Suggest to the doctor that your business "sponsor" a magazine rack. If the doctor doesn't already have a rack, you purchase an inexpensive rack and, in exchange, your business gets exclusive category rights to distribute its literature in the racks. Your information will garner a higher level of credibility when it sits among publications such as National Geographic, Time, Newsweek, WebMD Magazine, and important medical literature.

There are so many forms and variations of Out-of-home advertising that you could easily write a 500-page book on this medium alone. Suffice it to say that as you walk around outside or as you visit places outside of your home become attuned to what advertising is present. You will probably come up with a few inexpensive ideas of your own.

6. Internet - This has rapidly changed the face of business and literally the way we live our lives. You already know this and you are also aware that it continues to evolve at such a rapid pace that it is very difficult to keep up with all of it. Don't fret and don't try to keep up with everything because you can't. What you can do is look at the big picture, talk to some of the real pros and trendsetters that you may know or have access to and, occasionally, attend a webinar. Webinars are great for small businesses because you can attend them without leaving your office. Equally as important, many of them are free. So, you can learn a great deal about the Internet and the latest trends while you save time and money. Learning should be on going because the Internet and the next great "wave", Mobile computing, must be built into your business operations. If you do not embrace the Internet and Mobile communications you place the survival of your business in great peril.

Think of Mobile as the ability to do everything from watching TV to listening to the radio, to searching the Internet, to getting and sending email, and conducting much of your social and business activity without the need to be stationary. You can be on the go, traveling from one place to another and multi-tasking to your heart's content. Currently, the only thing holding Mobile back is adoption. With the advent of larger screen sizes (IPad), more tools and programs (apps and browser access /compatibility) and consumer understanding and acceptance, Mobile is a very big part of the future of business.

Regarding the Internet, here are some of the things that you must do as soon as humanly possible, if you haven't already implemented them:

- Website – If you do not have one, make it your first order of business. Actually, the first step is to choose and purchase a Web address (URL). Don't even print business cards until you have a URL and an individual business email address for yourself and any other key people in your company. Certain businesses try to get by with Google, Yahoo or an AOL address, but that sends a signal that your business is home-based or, worse-yet, part-time and "less than professional".

There are reputable companies that can design your website for as little as $500. This is an area where it can really pay off to shop around. A $500 website may suffice for the moment, but it may not serve you well enough if you experience the growth that you hope for. It may only cost you an additional $1,000 to $2,000 to get a significantly better website that makes a "big" statement about your services and leads to far more sales.

- Search Engine Optimization (SEO) – Unlike the movie, "Field of Dreams", you cannot simply build your website and have potential customers come in droves. Marketing your website is important if you want to generate leads from potential customers performing online searches. SEO is one of the least costly means at your disposal. I know marketers who do SEO for themselves. If you do not have the time or the inclination to learn SEO and perform regular maintenance, there are many capable companies that specialize in this area.

- Paid Search / Online lead-generation companies – There are hundreds of companies in the business of acquiring and selling leads to businesses of all sizes in virtually every category you can think of. It is likely that you have used one or more of these, either as a consumer "shopping around" or as a business seeking new leads. Some of these companies are very well known such as AT&T YellowPages.com, SuperYellowPages.com, Service Magic, eLocal Listing, Merchant Circle, and, of course, Google, Yahoo and Bing.

Paid search is absolutely worth testing. You may prefer to do it yourself via a service such as Google Ad words or you may prefer something more turnkey, such as ReachLocal, a company that can plan and implement the program for you.

Here's the thing to keep in mind about Paid Search: you only pay when a potential customer clicks on your ad and visits your landing page and/or website. That visit may or may not generate a lead in the form of a phone call, contact form completion or other means of capturing the potential customer's information. On the other hand, if you work with a lead generation company, they will supply you with leads.

The amount that you pay for a lead can vary greatly depending on which lead-generation company you use. For example, if you use YellowPages.com for telephone call leads, your cost-per-lead may be relatively high (e.g. $25.00) versus Service Magic.com (e.g. $15.00). However, you may find that the quality of the leads generated by YellowPages is superior and results in more sales than the leads from Service Magic. Again, the aforementioned is only a hypothetical example, not a recommendation. The point to bear in mind is that the quality of the lead is ultimately more important than the cost of the lead.

The most important thing to do with Paid Search and Lead Generation services is keep good records of the number of leads, cost per lead, number of sales and total amount of each sale generated, so that you can perform an on-going analysis and improvement of your online lead generating activities. You must have a "test and refine" mentality.

- Social Media – The great thing about Social Media is that a small business can gain a significant presence for free. Three of the major Social Media, Facebook (a social networking site), Twitter (a microblog), and LinkedIn (a business-oriented social networking site) are a great starting point for most businesses. They are all free on the basic service level. YouTube, is another free marketing tool at your disposal. If you can develop videos that feature your business and will be of interest to potential customers or existing customers, than YouTube makes sense.

Many marketing experts feel that the aforementioned Social Media are not the most effective means of reaching the online community for free. There are those who argue that blogs, online reviews, forum threads, and a press and media campaign will garner better results. These are all excellent tools. Some are free, while others will require a budget to do them correctly. Let's face it, most small businesses don't have the time to do an effective Public Relations effort, nor would many know where to start. However, there are very capable writers and PR companies with reasonable rates ready to help small businesses.

Social Media is all the rage at the moment. Don't overreact to the hype and understand what SM can and cannot do for a small business. It is more suited to customer relationship management than it is to acquiring new customers. It is great for carrying on a dialogue with your existing customers. You can let them know about new services/products and special offers and coupons. You can engage them on a one-on-one basis and get great feedback from them. This will lead to product improvements and increased sales from existing customers because you have formed a more intimate bond with them. Let's face it, current and past customers are your best advocates if they like you. In this way, Social Media will indirectly lead to new customers.

7. Email – Opt-in email campaigns to current customers as well as efforts directed to potential customers via third-party lists have proven to be very effective. If your current customer base is small and you do not want to invest in purchasing an email list here are ways to build a list of your own:

- Link to a sign-up form that is on your Web site by including the link in your email signature line

- Promote your online sign-up page in your brochures and other sales collateral

- Conduct a contest or drawing to encourage people to sign up

- Put a newsletter subscription URL on the footer of catalogs or printed newsletters

- Feature the newsletter subscription URL on print ads or on bill stuffers

- Promote sign up via telephone messaging while on hold and voice mail

- Link to event registration, online donation to charities or any other activity that provides the opportunity to promote a sign-up

- Include a sign-up offer it in your shopping cart mechanism

- Create a face-to-face sign-up sheet at your store, events, trade shows or while networking

- Allow people to forward your communications to others via a "forward this newsletter to others" option in your email communication

- Promote the newsletter via Paid Search

- Use Search Engine Optimization to drive sign-ups

- Send direct mail highlighting the online discussion. Mention that you are offering some incentives or discounts via e-mail only

- Offer opt-in incentives - Discounts or access to white papers and/or special reports

- Hand out sign-up forms at speaking engagements and seminars

- Collect business cards with e-mails on them at trade show booths

- Make changing an email address easy. Try to allow for subscribers to update the address on their own

- Require an email address when people register for event

Chapter 31

General Selling Skills

By Paul L. Morris

This chapter is primarily intended for those selling products and services to businesses where long term relationships are crucial but many of the suggestions and approaches outlined here will apply to most selling situations including retail and professional services, you are primarily selling yourself. Naturally, your approach will vary depending on what it is you are selling.

Though much of this chapter deals with basic selling concepts, even those who have been out there selling for a while should be able to pick up some pointers. I myself am always on the lookout for better and more innovative ways to improve my selling skills and knowledge.

This topic can easily fill one or more books, but since I have been given about ten pages to work with many ideas are summarized and condensed. I have endeavored though to emphasize those points I believe to be essential in improving your skills in sales in order to close mores sales, get more business and make more money with less time and effort. I caution you though, that while using these principles will help you sell better they must be applied conscientiously to be affective, which means, cutting corners and being lazy won't make it happen.

Selling, like any other skill-set, can be learned and even mastered if you want it badly enough and get the proper training. It never ceases to amaze me how people assume that one can sell or even sell well without proper training. What is even more surprising is how bewildered the owner or boss of a small to medium sized enterprise is when the "salesman" (the one who was told to sell, though untrained, thus unprepared for the task) often fails. Yes there are some people who just have the knack for selling, typically those with great people skills and a lot of guts but even those exceptions can be helped to increase their closing percentages with proper training.

Please do not fall prey to the idea that when you sell you "bother" people and thus selling is a bad or negative thing and those who do it are not nice people. Selling makes the world go round, yes that and love too. A competent and honest sales person is the consumer's best friend. Just think back to your most enjoyable buying experiences. I wager that they were facilitated buy pleasant and competent sales people. Also sales can provide a nice comfortable living for those who do it well. So let's see what it takes to succeed.

DISCOMFORT AROUND THE SELLING PROCESS

There are usually two main reasons why people are uncomfortable selling. I can't tell you how many times in the training business I have heard people say these words: I hate selling! The reasons people feel this way are first they believe those who tell them selling is not nice because you bother people and because they just don't know how to sell. Well heck who wouldn't be uncomfortable doing something that they are unprepared for and didn't know how to do? Therefore when you learn what you're doing and how to do it, it doesn't seem quite so scary anymore.

Believe me there were few people who were less scared than I was when I started out selling computers products and services in the late 1970's. And if I weren't confident of my technical knowledge (I was a computer programming and systems manager when I switched to selling) I would not have tried it at all. But I had a burning desire to be successful in sales and worked very hard to learn what I needed to know to do well in my new vocation. Bye the way, if you truly want to succeed in selling let this chapter be just the beginning of your studies; also read books, listen to books on CD and take courses that can improve your skill and knowledge. That's what I did and it helped a lot.

ATTITUDE, APPROACH and MINDSET

You must believe that you are helping the prospect otherwise you are trying to sell something that you don't believe in and that should never be the case. Without conviction you are doomed to fall short. This does not mean that it is impossible sell something that you don't have a passion for, it just means that if you want to excel, sell something you at least like and preferably love.

Always Control What is Controllable from your end (there are more than enough things that you can't control). In other words: be neat and well groomed, be punctual, be prepared, follow up, always be true to your word, be honest, practice your pitch and so on. Oh yes, and always follow up!

You Must Maintain Control Of The Sale! You know how to sell your products and services far better than the prospect knows how to buy them. Why leave it to them to buy, when it's your job to sell! When you lose control of the sale, you lose the sale! should be your mantra. Don't you maintain control when you're creating your product or service or do you leave it up to chance? Why should selling be any different? Would you prefer to leave the outcome of the sale to chance? You must guide the prospect through the sales process. Whether you know it or not the prospect is relying on you to do just that; to take them through the steps of the sale. The less you are in control, the harder you make it for the prospect to buy. The prospect expects you to be his/her leader in this process, so don't let him/her down. Don't worry, if they don't want what you are selling, they won't buy it. You are not being mean by closing the deal, you are simply making it easy for them to get something they need. I can't emphasize this point enough. Just be pleasantly persistent.

Make it Easy for Them to Buy every step of the way. Never ask your prospect (or customer) to do something that you can do for them — within reason. Don't ever expect them to know "how to buy" it is your responsibility to "know how to sell." Always make it clear about what exactly they are buying (what they can expect from you and what is expected of them). And after the sale, always check in on a regular basis to see how they are doing.

You sell in this order: 1) Yourself, 2) Your company and 3) Your product or service. Trust me prospects are not even vaguely interested in buying what you are offering until they know who they are buying from (that means you and your company).

How to Sell Yourself.

People buy from:

- People they like (see below The Method, Creating rapport)
- People they trust (most prospects do not know very much about the product/service that they are buying, that is why their trust and belief in your word is so important). People they believe care about their satisfaction
- People who know their product or service (who know what they are talking about)

How To Sell Your Company (see below, The Sales Process. Gaining Acceptance)

Prospects want to know that:

- Your company has a solid reputation
- Your company has been around awhile
- They are reliable
- They take care of your customers
- Will remain in business

How to Sell Your Product/Service

The prospect will truly consider your product/service only when the first two criteria are met. After all would you buy anything of any value that you expected to keep for a while without considering if the company you buy from had a decent history of performance, supported their product and was expected to stay in business for a while? **Mention Features but Sell Benefits.** Features get people excited and are fun to discuss but it's how these features will ultimately benefit the prospective buyer that will in the end make or break the sale. Many sales people don't bother connecting features to benefits because they don't get the concept, realize it is necessary, are being lazy or believe that the features connection to a benefit is all too obvious and does not need to be discussed. Well even if the connection were obvious (and let me tell you from many years of selling it is often far from the case) emphasizing and reinforcing the point of that benefit is essential in closing the sale. And remember that connection (feature to benefit) naturally seems obvious to the seller because she or he knows it so well but typically the buyer does not know very much about it and if she/he does it never hurts to remind them. Plus, people always appreciate a good thorough sales presentation. It says something about you and your company.

Always tune in to channel WIFM (What's In it For Me) from the prospects point of view.

Always Ask Open Ended Questions (which cannot be answered yes or no).

The reason for this is that you want the prospect to talk as much as possible. The more he/she talks the more you will learn about them, their situation, their needs and thus how to sell to them. Good listening skills is one of the most important keys to good selling skills. AND NEVER INTERUPT YOUR PROSPECT WHEN HE OR SHE IS SPEAKING! If you have a burning question or comment, jot it down and wait until the person is finished speaking (I naturally assume you carry some type of writing pad and variety of pens with you when you go out on a sales call) then say it. Also, if you don't write it down then you most likely are not paying enough attention to what your prospect is saying because you are waiting to speak and paying more attention to what you have to say and not totally listening and that is a turn off and ultimately unproductive in a selling situation.

Never Lie To A Prospect

If you don't know an answer, tell them that we can: A. Address that at the meeting, if you are in the process of setting up an appointment (this is covered in more detail below) or B. During a meeting tell them that you will get back to them soon with the answer they require.

Never assume anything when you can ask or otherwise find out the answer. It is amazing how certain you can be about something and then find out your assumption is wrong! I cannot begin to tell you how many times this has happened to me until I finally learned my lesson. And make no mistake, this can be a very co$tly lesson to learn.

Always know the expected outcome of each meeting and contact with your prospect or customer otherwise you are wasting her/his time and yours as well. If you don't take your business, yourself and your time seriously, then don't expect anyone else to take it seriously either!

Always get agreement on the next step before ending a meeting or phone conversation with your customer or prospect. This is how you keep the ball rolling. One of the reasons I am writing this chapter is to teach the reader, if he/she doesn't already know, what the steps are in the selling process. Selling is not and should never be guess work; it is a process that when properly followed will often lead to a sale. You should always know for each selling situation where you are at and what the next steps are that need to be taken to get to and close the sale.

If you are contacted by a prospect or a customer about a problem do not assume you know what it is. For if you suggest a problem that they do not already know about, it will be an additional problem to the one they called about. Instead just ask what it is. Be very cautious about making assumptions!

THE SALES PROCESS IN THREE MAIN STEPS:

Setting the appointment, Gaining acceptance (the meeting), and Closing the sale

Setting The Appointment (cold calling over the phone or face to face).

In order for the prospect to listen to your "value proposition" you must first gain his/her attention. I guarantee that when you call a decision maker she/he is thinking about anything but you and what you have to say. Most sales people miss this one and though it may seem somewhat trivial, let me assure you that it is not. If you fail to capture the prospect's full attention then your chances of convincing him or her to give up their valuable time to see you in person is greatly diminished.

Getting prospects attention:

- Ask a question (e.g., would you like to know how much our average client saved using our product/service last year?)
- A startling statement (our product/service can cut the cost of running your office by as much as…)
- The third party opener (someone he/she knows)
- Talk about something he/she is interested in
- The mystery opener – arouse their curiosity
- The famous person or big name opener (so & so says this is one of the best products/services he/she ever used).
- The complement (be sincere and accurate and not just fawning)
- The news flash (this can be very affective if the news is about her/his industry and will affect the way they do business)

Creating interest AKA the Value proposition

In this step you tell your prospect why she/he should be interested in your product/service so that he/she will take the time to set up a meeting with you.

- Tell what she/ he will gain by buying from you
- What they will lose if they don't
- Speak in terms of features and benefits
- If they ask a question that you either do not know the answer to or don't want to get into at that moment just tell the person that this will be covered at the meeting in as much detail as the prospect wants.

Gaining Acceptance: at the meeting (Who you are/What you've done/Who are your clients/What they say about you/Discuss/Present/Demonstrate your Product or Service)

Always be on time – in fact come early

Be neat (you women know what to do and you guys dress properly, make sure your clothes are clean and pressed and shine you shoes. No one likes being in the company of a slovenly person.)

What to bring to the meeting: Note pad, plenty of pens (some in red or other colors and even markers to emphasize certain information), appointment calendar, contracts (even if you don't expect to close then and there), brag book (details below), and any other equipment you need for presentation like samples, computers, etc.

Brag book: Purpose of brag book is to establish that you and your company are worth doing business with (see How To Sell Your Company above).

Brag book should be a nice looking three hole binder, leather bound if possible and should contain:

- Copies of diplomas & Certificates
- Letters (Testimonials, appointments and awards)
- Press clippings
- Publications (books & articles)
- Pictures (with you and prominent people)
- Sample pictures of what you sell
- Come around the desk or prospects side of the table and leaf through it with them pointing things out and explaining what is being looked at.

Presentation/Demonstration of product or service

- Make certain the decision maker is present (if that is impossible try to at least meet with them face to face before leaving their office).
- Always make certain that prospect is following each point by asking what they think about it and if they have any questions so far.
- Ask questions pertaining to prospects wants, needs and hot buttons.
  - Make certain you show them the thing(s) that they are most interested in.

- Recap at end to get their overall impression and what they like most and least (this will allow you to understand better how to close when the time comes)

The Close

If you have shown the prospect what he/she needs to see and know in order to make a decision, then you have earned the right to ask for his/her business. After a while this should become second nature. If the prospect makes a closing statement proceed to close.

Build Passion in you prospect: (Create a positive picture in their mind of the benefits you've outlined)

- Speak of how it would feel for him/her to be using your product/service.
- Ask him/her how they would be using your product/service.
- Have them discuss how things would be better after your product/service is being used in their organization.

Closing Commitment

Now, go right to that agreement that you put on her/his desk, just before you began to close.

Go through the agreement making certain that you have answered all his questions (ask "do you have any (other) questions?")

If he says no, you say "all you have to do is to authorize (sign) the agreement and we can get started.

Attempt to close each time you overcome an objection.

If your contact is not the final decision maker or is not the only decision maker try to meet the other(s) yourself with your contact so you can sell the other(s) as well and not leave it up to your contact to do your selling for you. Offer to be at the meeting with other decision makers in order to assist your contact in his/her presentation of your proposal.

When the prospect tells you that he/she is ready to buy you should immediately stop talking (even if you are in the middle of explaining something) and execute your closing procedure (e.g., get documents signed, obtain check, get verbal commitment, etc). If you keep talking all you can accomplish is the talk yourself out of a sale.

After the buying decision has been made, do not "muddy the waters" by introducing other alternatives, even if attractive, for this may unduly delay or kill your sale. In stead execute the sale and introduce the additional options at a later date when the customer has received the goods or services and you have been paid.

THE METHOD

Creating Rapport

When: Rapport should be established on the phone, at the meeting and continued at each contact. How much up front chitchat depends on how much the prospect enjoys small talk before getting down to business. But regardless of your prospect's personality type (weather he/she enjoys small talk or not) rapport must be re-established each time.

How: Find common ground: Try to find something that you both have in common (where they live, grew up, went to school, sports, travel, music, the military, art, movies, food and drink, family, or just the fact that you both like to "get down to business," etc.).

Show interest in what they do or like: Listen carefully when they speak and NEVER interrupt (take notes if necessary). If you are in their office look around to see his/her trophies, pictures, books, memorabilia, etc.

Overcoming objections (Always try to close after overcoming an objection)

Never get defensive when asked a difficult question, instead turn it around and tell him/her that you are glad they asked you this question and phrase your response in a positive way (not in a negative or defensive way.)

Example 1: Prospect - You charge too much!

Response: I'm glad that you brought that up. In fact, my customers view my work as an investment in their business. Because, their clients are so happy with results their business increases and it more than pays for their investment.

So instead of costing them money, I make them money. And I can make you money as well. (At this point, show the prospect testimonial letters saying where you've made money for your customers.)

Example 2: Prospect - You charge too much!

Response: I would rather explain price once than apologize for quality forever.

Feel, Felt, Found technique: Customer Objection, Response: I understand how you feel, others have felt the same way, but here is what they found...

If you get stumped by an objection, do the best you can and later think about it (or ask someone else) until you can come up with a good response and then record it for future reference.

Try to get them to talk about why they need your product or service.

Example 3: Prospect - You charge too much!

Response: Are you speaking about cost or value, because if you a talking about value...Now you are in control of the discussion. Then discuss your cost justification for his purchase.

At a meeting where you may close the deal. Lay a copy of agreement down in front of prospect. (If asked say "I just don't want to forget to go over it with you later")

Note: If he asks you to go over the agreement now (closing signal) or at any time during your presentation, STOP whatever you are doing and go over the agreement with him and CLOSE the deal! (What he is saying at this point is "I'm convinced [conviction step over, I already have the desire], I'm ready to buy.)

Closing questions you ask:

Definition: A question that you ask and when answered indicates the prospects interest in buying.

Examples: When would you like delivery/installation of this product/service? When would you like/need to get started? What color/size/type/power rating do you require? How many people will be using the system? And so forth.

When prospect answers the question, you assume the sale and proceed as though he/she said "I want to buy." (i.e., go to your paperwork [agreement] and perform other tasks to conclude the sale)

If prospect stops you by not answering the question and says that he/she did not say that they were ready to commit to this purchase, then ask: what more do you need to know, see, experience before making that decision? And when that is satisfied, go back and try to close again. Continue in this manner until the deal is either closed or you find out why he/she is not ready to buy.

Closing signals from the prospect:

Definition: A closing signal is something the prospect does or says that indicates her/his interest in buying.

Examples: How soon can I have it? What colors does it come in? If he/she suddenly seems a little nervous or vulnerable (the nervousness indicates that they are vulnerable to buying).

After receiving a closing signal, stop whatever you are doing, even if you are in the middle of a sentence and close the deal. Example: How soon can I have it? Response: If we can take care of the paper work (contract) and you can get me a down payment check today, you can have it in…

THE MEETING (PRESENTATION / DEMONSTRATION)

The Setup

Get the decision maker involved by making certain that he/she is present. (If that is not possible and you decide to have the meeting anyway, try to at least meet the decision maker face to face afterward while you are at their location). Note: If the decision maker is not willing to be at the meeting this means that you have failed to establish enough interest in your product/service and should re-evaluate the situation.

Establish the amount of time and resources you require (if established over the phone email to confirm)

Call or email a day or two before the call to remind the prospect of the meeting

The Call in General

Be early (If you are running late call to alert the prospect).

If you arrive late, apologize only once and get on with the meeting.

Shake everyone's hand and give them your card and introduce your technical person (if any) and make certain he/she gives out their cards.

Write down everyone's name and title (function) and memorize if possible. (Check out "The Memory Book" by Harry Lorayne and Jerry Lucas for remembering names.)

At the beginning of the each meeting confirm how much time you have been allotted so that you are not caught short. Sometimes things change at the last minute.

They will be more receptive if you show a genuine interest in what they are doing and how they do it. Try to get your prospect to give you a tour of her/his facility, etc.

Presentation / Demonstration

Use Accelerated Learning principles for presentation format (separate course)

In general create Receptivity (Openness) and Engagement (Involvement). Show pictures and try to get the prospect to touch or sample the product.

They will be engaged if you involve them in the presentation/demonstration by gearing meeting to their interests and having them become as "hands on" as possible. (Examples: Test driving a car and typing on the keyboard of a PC or tasting a food product.)

Keep checking to make certain they understand and are following the information being presented. If there are two or more "presenters" in attendance, the one not active should be watching the prospects to gauge their reaction (i.e., are they following, lost, interested, bored, etc.) Ask "Any questions?" "What do you think about this feature? How important is that feature to you?" etc. Solicit comments at the end. Ask if there is anything else they need to see or know about your products/services. If the answer is no, nothing then do a trial close.

COLD CALLING

Always find out as much as possible about the person and company you are calling on.

Use these and other resources:

- The company website
- Annual report
- The internet in general
- Someone who knows the company
- Get friendly with someone in the company

Qualify your Prospect

Make certain that the person you are speaking to is not just a tire kicker. You can establish this by asking the following questions: When do you need to get the product/service and what budget do you have for it or how much were you looking to spend. Also, who is the decision maker (Will there be anyone else involved in making this decision?)

If someone else is involved in the decision making process make certain that they are present when you make your pitch and demonstration (this point is crucial!).

Calling in Person

Ask receptionist for prospect by name, if he/she asks if you know them always tell the truth.

If receptionist or prospect's secretary says that you need an appointment, say "fine" and try to set up an appointment on the spot.

If you get through to the prospect or secretary have a compelling reason why prospect should see you now.

Calling by Phone

The purpose of the call is not to sell your products/services but to set up the meeting (unless you are selling over the phone), so always sell to the next step.

If you do not get through, leave a message and send an email with your information. Never give ALL the information but just enough to create interest. They will be filled in at the meeting. The purpose of this contact is not to give the prospect all your information but to get a meeting!

If you get through use attention and interest generating remarks (see Getting prospects attention / Creating interest above, for details)

Answer initial questions establishing who you are, what you sell and your credentials in this area and industry, any detail questions about product/service should be addressed at the meeting. Use these detail questions to sell the meeting by saying "we can answer all these questions and more at the meeting."

Keep following up until you get the meeting or they convince you that they are not qualified as a prospect.

In conclusion: Get the appointment, give the presentation that is convincing and close the deal. Good luck and good selling!

Chapter 32

Cold Calling Tips For Business Owners and Sales Professionals

By Deborah Anderson

The most successful tips:

Be a good listener, respond accordingly. Adjust your tone to mirror the other person's. Do not take negative reaction personally. You don't know if you just caught that person running to the phone after spilling their coffee and were just annoyed at that and not necessarily anything that you had to say.

Approach every dial as a brand new opportunity! Do not let the last call's negativity affect the next call.

Having a positive attitude really does shine through in the tone of your voice. Keeping a smile on your face even though they cannot see it will also shine through.

Attitude is EVERYTHING. When someone is only "meeting" you over the phone their senses are heightened just like a blind person's other senses are more acute. How you come across over the phone is their entire impression of you.

How you introduce yourself leaves an everlasting impression throughout the entire conversation and it creates the tone leading up to your call's objective. It also directs the conversation and is a guideline which will lead you to your ultimate goal for that call.

1. peak slowly and deliberately. Think more carefully than if you were in person.
2. Watch your Um's and Ah's, try to sound relaxed.
3. Always be courteous, regardless of the prospect or clients reaction. Never hang up on anyone.
4. Be sure to provide a phone number where they can call you back. It is a Federal Law.
5. Take notes. This way, when someone says to call them back, you have a more familiar tone with which to start off the return call. As an example — Fred says call me after I get back from my vacation in Hawaii so when you do call back you can ask how was his trip and more details to relax him which will lower his guard, such as which islands did he visit?
6. Get a headset or Bluetooth so you never "put the receiver down".
7. Expect to make 20 – 30 calls per hour.
8. Never leave a message. Hang up after 3 rings.

Think of selling as helping to solve someone's problem. In telemarketing, you are always trying to find the people who have that problem.

The DO NOT CALL list: When they ask you to put them on the list — make sure that you do not call them back! The fine can be as high as $11,000 per offense if they choose to press charges.

- If the prospect asks to be put on the "do not call list" — Say "I am sorry to have bothered you", and make a "list".
- For consumer lists — ensure you buy a "scrubbed list". This is the responsibility of the list company you buy your list from. Ask for details that the list was scrubbed quarterly.
- Top Recommended list company: Info USA.

IN SUMMARY - Sales is a numbers game. View every rejection as one less you need to experience before your next call or sale. Expect objections and have your rebuttals ready. Listen and try to learn from each rejection and use it as an opportunity to improve.

Chapter 33

How To Use Social Media To Boost Your Business

By Marie Griffin

There are many reasons you should take advantage of the popular social media platforms of LinkedIn, Twitter and Facebook, but one reason I reject is "everybody's doing it." If you simply succumb to pressure from well-meaning friends, relatives or colleagues—and don't have your own plans and goals—you may do your business more harm than good.

Just like a retail store, a Facebook page, LinkedIn profile or Twitter account is a setting where business may occur, but social media success requires your presence and effort on an ongoing basis. You wouldn't open on Main Street and only show up on opening day, would you?

For a business or businessperson, Facebook, Twitter, and LinkedIn will enable you to broadcast information to people who have agreed to view your messages by liking (Facebook) or following (LinkedIn and Twitter) your business or connecting with you (LinkedIn). However, unlike traditional broadcast media, social media allows the recipients of your messages to add something by liking them, commenting on them, and sharing them.

These platforms also take the age-old practices of word-of-mouth recommendations and personal endorsements and magnify them—making them incrementally more powerful. When one of your followers shares your message, photo or video, their followers may do the same and your content could "go viral," that is, spread from friend to friends to friends of friends until hundreds, thousands or, potentially, millions of people are reached. Worldwide, Facebook had 1.39 billion monthly active users (MAUs) as of December 31, 2014; LinkedIn reached 300 million members in April, 2014, and Twitter averaged at 288 million MAUs during the fourth quarter of 2014.

If you don't want to reach millions or even thousands, social media is extremely effective in communicating to a small target audience. Regardless of the size of your business, one of the biggest benefits of social media is the ease with which you can reach a group of people simultaneously with a single message—at no cost.

It is free to set up an account on Facebook, LinkedIn and Twitter, although all three sell advertising and LinkedIn also sells "premium" accounts with additional features for a monthly fee. In this chapter, I will be covering the free features only.

Below, I will provide some basic information on the three popular social networks of Facebook, Twitter and LinkedIn, and I'll suggest some ways you can use them to increase your business. But please remember that you will need to develop a plan for how you will use each of these tools on an ongoing basis. It won't help your business to open an "office" on social media and leave it vacant.

Before setting up shop on any social network, your job is to answer the following questions:
- Which network or networks are most appropriate for my business?
- What are my goals with each one?
- Who is going to be responsible for updating my Facebook and LinkedIn pages and sending out "tweets" on Twitter? How often?
- Who will respond to messages and comments that come from these platforms?
- How do I plan to build my audience of Friends, Connections and Followers—and who will be responsible?

- How will I continue to educate myself about social media so that I can take advantages of new networks, features and functions as they come along?

FACEBOOK: Make the most of the No. 1 social networking site

Don't assume Facebook is only for young people; the fastest-growing subset of Facebook users is aged 45 and up. And, even though Facebook is no longer as "cool" as it once was among teenagers, it's one of the first places they go to find things out, such as the hours for your store, your business' location, or whether you are offering discounts or coupons.

If you haven't already set up a company page on Facebook, your first task is to find out how your customers use the social network. Ask them during one-to-one meetings and/or send out a survey. (You can do this for free on the Web using SurveyMonkey.) While you have their attention, ask them what they would like your company to do or offer on Facebook. It's also important to look at your competitors' Facebook pages. How do you want to differentiate yourself from them? What are they doing that you might want to try?

Next, think about your messages to potential customers; what advertising vehicles, promotions and types of events have you used to get customers in your history so far? Again, think of Facebook as a way to amplify the tactics you've already used successfully. To set up a Facebook page, you only need three things, an email address and two pieces of art. Unlike a website that you might have to pay someone to design for you, a Facebook page is already formatted. The "header" portion at the top of each page has room for one large wide image and one smaller square image. If you have a logo, the small square spot is ideal for it. If you are a service provider—lawyer, doctor, consultant or message therapist—display a portrait of yourself. Even if you have a logo, a photo of you will form a more personal relationship, the kind that Facebook is designed to enhance.

The larger image, called the cover photo, will measure 851 x 315 pixels. Those dimensions may not mean anything to you and they don't have to. What you need to know is that the image will be between 2 ½ and 3 times wider than it is high; the ratio is the same as a photo 2 inches high and 5.4 inches wide. If you're taking a photo, use the horizontal (wide) view and remember that the image will be cropped—Facebook does this automatically—to the full width but only half the height. The outside of your building might work; your stately front door probably won't.

Also for the top of your page, you will use a pull-down menu to choose a category for your business, such as Companies & Organizations, Brands & Products or Local Business, and the type of business you have, such as Health/Wellness, Recreation/Sports or Teens/Kids.

The most important elements of the page are the ones you write yourself, the "About" information and its accompanying "Description," which can include your company's website address.

The Description must be short. I suggest you search Facebook for companies you like—or those with which you compete—for ideas. For example, here's Crate and Barrel's description: "Live the Crate and Barrel lifestyle with our exclusive collection of home furnishings and housewares classic to contemporary."

Once you've created your page, what will you post there? People generally like discounts and many companies will put sales and special promotions on their Facebook pages, but start small. Remember that a really good promotion could go viral, so you must have enough product in stock and be able to afford a high redemption rate. Consider a gift-with-purchase promotion where you can control the cost of the gift and not sacrifice your margins.

Fortunately, sales and promotions are not the only option. Is there any helpful information you can give your customers? Let's say you're a CPA offering income tax preparation. You might post reminders about important filing dates and deadlines. If you have a veterinary practice, you can post helpful tips like "Five signs your cat isn't feeling well."

The Facebook page for Magnolia Bakery, a New York City retailer that is expanding into other markets, is an excellent example of how to create demand without dropping prices. One post showed a spectacular photo of a cupcake sitting next to a fresh sliced lemon. The copy said, "Need an afternoon pick me up? Stop by for our cupcake of the day: Lemon. Pucker up!"

Research has shown that photos and videos get more attention than text updates on Facebook so include them whenever you can.

Never forget the interactivity that's built into your Facebook page. You want people to like your posts, leave positive comments, and share your business-building offers. On the other side of the coin, though, you might not like some of the comments. Offensive, off-color comments can be immediately deleted but some comments that aren't positive might present an opportunity. If you are willing and able, you can make a comment to dispute incorrect information or resolve a commenter's problem. Many social media experts believe it is better to "engage" with unhappy customers—and perhaps turn them around—than to ignore a legitimate opinion or complaint.

How do you build an audience? Facebook enables you to send email invitations to lists of people using most popular email programs. Include "Like us on Facebook" signs in your business location and on all employees' business cards. Include a connection to your Facebook page from your website. Add information about your Facebook page to the bottom of all your emails. Include your Facebook page on all the advertising you do, both online and offline. Facebook also offers advertising programs to help.

For more tips and help, Facebook has created pages for business users, including areas where you can get help to get started (www.facebook.com/business).

LINKEDIN: Mine a pipeline of people who can buy, influence, and hire

LinkedIn bills itself as the world's largest professional network on the Internet; two-thirds of its members are now located outside the

United States. Your relationship to LinkedIn starts with your personal profile, essentially an online resume. It's up to you to decide which jobs, schools and volunteer experiences to include, so you could decide to leave out parts of your career that are no longer relevant or too long ago (if you're concerned about revealing your age).

The profile format features a place for your photo. Use it. Although LinkedIn is not a dating service—and you should use a photo of yourself in professional clothing and a businesslike setting—LinkedIn is designed to connect businesspeople. Your photo will enhance your ability to make these connections.

As an individual businessperson on LinkedIn, you are able to invite other LinkedIn members to connect with you and other members can message you to ask to connect. LinkedIn lets you make these invitations using its system, so you do not have to know or enter your potential connection's email address.

When you find someone on LinkedIn with whom you would like to connect, click the connect button and you will be presented with a list of possible ways you may know that person, including friend, colleague, classmate, or "We've done business together." If you indicate the person is a colleague or "we've done business," you will see a pull-down menu listing all the companies you've worked at, according to your profile. If you know Peter Pumpkin from selling him x-ray machines when you were a representative for Medical Devices Inc., you would check your employer, Medical Devices Inc., from the menu. If you indicate Peter was a colleague, LinkedIn will check to make sure both you and Peter listed the same company in your profiles.

You will also see the option, "I don't know Peter." If you click that box, you'll get a pop-up admonition from the LinkedIn system, saying, "Invitations should only be sent to people you know personally. LinkedIn values our users' privacy and responds to complaints about unwelcome invitations."

However, that message does not mean you have reached a dead end. In fact, one of the most powerful functions of LinkedIn is to connect you to businesspeople you don't know by way of the people you do know. People in your personal LinkedIn network are defined by the number of degrees of separation there are between the two of you. Your contacts are first-degree connections. If you and another LinkedIn member are 2nd-degree connections, you will have at least one person in common and that person's name will be displayed. If you want to connect with Peter Pumpkin because he is a potential client or employer or mentor, you can use LinkedIn to ask that mutual contact to introduce you.

Because of the way LinkedIn profiles are set up, LinkedIn is commonly used by people looking for new jobs and human resources professionals looking for new employees. As a result, job advertising is responsible for about half of LinkedIn's total revenue.

However, LinkedIn, which became a public company in May 2011, is seeking to become a business networking site for purposes beyond the job search. Part of that effort is the Company Pages feature inspired by Facebook. You must be a LinkedIn member with a personal profile at least 50% complete to set up a Company Page. Also, you must be currently working at the company according to your LinkedIn profile and you need to have an email address that relates to the company name, as opposed to a Gmail, Yahoo! mail or MSN account.

LinkedIn members can choose to "follow" companies and companies can send free messages to any members that have chosen to follow them. In addition to job openings, LinkedIn executives hope companies will send messages about new products and services, financial updates, and other relevant information for businesspeople. Eventually, LinkedIn would like to be considered "the Facebook for business," that is, the primary platform businesses use to communicate with clients, customer and prospects.

Another major feature of LinkedIn is LinkedIn Groups, which allow you to interact with people who share your business interests. There are roughly 4 million groups now on the network. Some groups are open, which means any LinkedIn member can join.

Others require that the group administrator accepts your request to join. Once you become a group member, you are allowed to start discussions or contribute to them. This is another way to make connections with other people in your field, including potential customers, employees or decision makers who can influence your business. It's also a great way to establish yourself as an expert among your peers. However, like other social networks, your ability to make use of LinkedIn Groups is related to the effort and time you're willing to put in. One more piece of advice: LinkedIn aren't the place to post unsolicited sales pitches. You'll be asked to stop and, if you don't, you may be kicked out.

To try to bring users to LinkedIn on a daily basis, the platform has added professional content in the form of LinkedIn Pulse, which includes a news feed that you can personalize according to your business interests; posts from high-profile "influencers" such as Microsoft founder Bill Gates, popular spiritual leader Deepak Chopra, and Richard Branson, founder of the Virgin Group; and a blogging feature that allows LinkedIn members—including you—to write about their business interests and opinions. Your blog post will be presented in the news feeds of your connections, any of whom may choose to share your post more widely, which could increase your visibility incrementally among business leaders.

There's much more to learn about using LinkedIn. A place to start is the Help Center at http://help.linkedin.com.

TWITTER: Send a timely message in a "tweet" that's short and sweet

Twitter started as a way to automatically distribute short messages similar to text messages to large groups. It evolved into a worldwide service with an interesting catch—each message, known as a "tweet," is limited to 140 characters. You don't have to count characters yourself. As you write, you will see a small number in the messaging box letting you know how many characters you have used.

You need to know two things about Twitter vernacular. The @ sign is the first character in all usernames, whether the user is a person, such as @mariegriffin; a company, such as @microsoft, or a product, such as @tide for P&G's laundry detergent. The # sign, known as a hashtag, is a way users tag posts when they want to communicate with others about a certain topic, such as #news, #love, #fashion, #2016election, etc.

Similar to Facebook, each user gets a short profile. This includes space for a small portrait photo, logo or image; a larger wide image, and a pithy description of fewer than 160 characters. You can link to your website, if you have one, from the profile.

Your Twitter home page is your control panel. On the upper left-hand side you will find your user name, the number of tweets you have posted, the number of other Twitter users you are following, and the number of Twitter users following you. In the center of the page is the constantly updated feed of tweets from all of the people, products, and companies you follow. At the very top of that feed, next to your picture or whatever image you use to identify your Twitter account is a box with the words, "What's happening." Those words will disappear as soon as you move your curser into that area to post words or an image. Alternately, you can click a shaded box on the top right-hand side of the Twitter toolbar labeled Tweet and start composing.

Following and being followed is a core feature of Twitter. When you follow another user—person, company or product—that user's tweets will show up in your "stream," equivalent to a Facebook news feed. Your followers will see your tweets in their streams. When you see a message you like, you can mark it as a favorite, and if you want to share it, you can "retweet" it, that is, repost that message so that it can be seen by your followers. You can comment to the user who has posted a given tweeter by clicking reply. You can also send "direct messages," similar to text messages, to individual users who are following you.

Why use Twitter? It's a very efficient way to distribute timely information. If you're having a sale today or a special guest arriving at 3PM, a tweet is a great way to remind people. If your business is a service, such as consulting or financial planning, you can use

Twitter to make comments or suggestions that will remind your followers of your expertise. Tweet about your upcoming radio interview or the speech you're giving at an industry event. Tweet links to articles where you have been quoted or news stories that might be helpful to your clients or potential clients. If you follow people or information sources you respect, you can retweet anything you think your followers will find interesting or helpful.

One useful tip for keeping your messages under 140 characters is to link to a website, video or blog where your followers can get more information. In most cases, that will require that you use a "link shortener." These are tools that allow you to insert any web page address (called a URL) and receive a short unique string of letters and numbers that will direct people to the same page.

One popular URL shortener is bitly.com (previously spelled bit.ly), but there are others, including tinyURL.com, Su.pr, Lnk.co, t.co, Ow.ly and Goo.gl, the official URL shortener from Google. Link shorteners can also be used to manage the size of URLs you want to share on Facebook and LinkedIn.

How do you get your customers and potential customers to follow you on Twitter? Start by picking some organizations and people to follow. Anyone who you follow may reciprocate and decide to follow you. You will find all the popular news outlets on Twitter, from TV stations to newspapers to trade publications. These are good sources of breaking news, as well as information for retweets. In addition, Twitter makes automatic suggestions of users to follow based on your profile.

Once you have written or found content that will interest the people you want to reach, there are a few inside tricks to capture their attention. First, use photos or images, which perennially get the highest engagement. Also, drop the "names," which start with the @ character, of people you want to notice you. Congratulate @John_Client when he gets a promotion or thank @BearBrightCandy for following your account. Equally important is to use hashtags, such as #sale, #coupon, or #special, which are likely to get your post extra attention. If you want to mention another user in a tweet, don't start with the @sign unless you only want that user to see it; most people just put a period in front of the @ when it's the first character.

Outside of Twitter, make sure you promote your presence there by letting your contacts know your Twitter username, @username, and URL, which will be https://twitter.com/username. Ask people to "follow me on Twitter" through signs, business cards, your website, email signature, etc. Then, don't forget to use Twitter regularly—at minimum, three times a week.

Twitter has a Help Center at https://support.twitter.com. It's not nearly as extensive as Facebook's multiple user guides, but you will find everything you need to get started on Twitter there.

Chapter 34

Five LinkedIn Tricks To Double Your Sales

By Julbert Abraham

As our world is changing with technology, we are in a time where we do everything over the internet, which allows us to expand our reach. As business owners and sales executives are looking for different ways to connect with their target audience, I strongly believe that social media is, and will remain, a very powerful tool. In our current time, companies all over the world are doing business with each other using platforms like Twitter, Facebook, LinkedIn and Instagram, to name a few.

These platforms have allowed marketers not only to target certain groups of people, but to be able to do business internationally, contributing to our global economy. With that said, each platform is suitable for a specific target audience. If you are a business to consumer company, my suggestion is to use Facebook or Instagram to build value, populate content and bring awareness to your products or services. If you are a business to business company, my recommendation is to leverage the power of LinkedIn.

With that platform, you as a marketer, business owner, or sales executive have access to over 313 million professionals worldwide. You are not only able to reach out to people in the United States, but globally, which makes LinkedIn a very powerful platform for business. In this chapter, we are going to elaborate on five tips that can help business owners use LinkedIn to grow and expand their business.

These tips are:

1st Tip: Be Proactive on LinkedIn

What does that mean? There are a lot of us on the platform; however, not a lot of us are currently using the platform to its full capacity. We are not very active, we don't check it quite often, we don't have any contents, and most importantly, we are not using LinkedIn to expand our network.

2nd Tip: Have a reason for using the Platform

A lot of people joined LinkedIn because someone told them to, or someone said to them, "You need to be on there, because it's social media; you can find a job there if your business is not working out." We have to understand that LinkedIn is far more than a resume update site where you can find a job. It is a platform which you should have a purpose to join and use. Think about it: why would you use LinkedIn?

Is it to create a network of people that you know or trust?

Is it to sell your products or services?

Is it a platform where you can share your expertise?

Is it for its branding and awareness capabilities?

Or is it "all of the above"?

3rd Tip: Have a Strong Profile

Your LinkedIn Profile is one of the most important tools on the platform. Why?

Your LinkedIn profile is a marketing tool; it is a silent sales person that serves as you when you are not there. That said, I would strongly recommend that you take the time to update, have a professional photo on your profile, great value added content and make your profile a welcoming place to the world.

4th Tip: Build Valuable Connections

LinkedIn is a very powerful network. As a business owner, you need a network of people who like you, know you and trust you before they do business with you. It is very important to get to know your current connections and build relationship with them. You have the ability to create a network like none other. That said, you have the choice to create a network of potential clients, potential partners and friends. When you are on LinkedIn, spend your time wisely, getting to know your connections and build a strong relationship with them that will go beyond the platform.

5th Tip: Be a Resource

In order to grow your business on LinkedIn, you have to be a resource. You have to be able to add value by being a subject matter expert, by developing relationships and connecting people within your network with each other. You have to go beyond just reaching out to folks to ask them to buy your services; you have to become a person that can help your fellow connections. As in any network it is important to serve in order to be served. That said, the same apply on LinkedIn. Once you develop a relationship with your connections, you have to think outside of the box on how you are a value and benefit to them as they are to you.

Your LinkedIn connections are a network where you are able to share ideas with each other, build relationships, find ways that you can help each other in order to grow and generate business. The platform gives you the ability to reach anyone around the world; it is by far one of the best professional search engines at our present time.

DO NOT ABUSE IT, USE IT WISELY, AND YOU WILL BE REWARDED EXPONENTIALLY.

Chapter 35

Efficiency Tips to Save You Stress

By Rose Benson

This chapter is vital for those who are either planning to start a business or already own one, because it gives bookkeeper's perspective of what to do and what not to do. No two businesses are exactly alike. Operational procedures may need to be adjusted throughout the life of the business as it grows and accommodates the sales to the target market. The best piece of advice would be to educate oneself to maintain the most efficient bookkeeping system for a business. After all, money is the lifeline of business operations, and the management of it (or lack thereof) can make or break even the best business ventures.

When starting a business, construct a business plan. There are terrific resources on the web or local agencies like SCORE or SBA. Take the time to learn, and consider how the business will operate and what the budget requirements for the bookkeeping needs should be. Both of these elements should be included in the business plan, among other things.

The considerations for bookkeeping needs should include what type of accounting software would be sufficient to maintain the records. QuickBooks is by far the most commonly used software for small businesses. On the other hand, other businesses might find that Quicken Home and Office or industry-specific software would be best. Is there a need to keep track of inventory, payroll, customer jobs or time tracking? Finally, of course, it is always critical that the computer storing the software is reliable and has enough memory to store the required files.

Perhaps the new entrepreneur has a great concept for a business but is not knowledgeable with record keeping or numbers. At this point, it may be prudent to hire a bookkeeper to setup the business on the chosen software and train the owner (or whomever will be inputting the income and expenses of the business) to use this software. For example, a program like QuickBooks might seem overwhelming and a business may only require certain parts of the program to be utilized and appropriate for the business. Setting up the chart of accounts and COGS (cost of goods sold) needs to be properly constructed so Financial Statements like the Profit and Loss and the Balance Sheet will be accurate. If it is in the budget to pay an experienced bookkeeper to do periodic maintenance, it would afford the entrepreneur more time to focus on making money and growing the business.

After researching the anticipated bookkeeping needs, business owners should interview some prospective bookkeepers to ask educated questions and have them supply an idea of cost so these figures can be included in the business plan. Everybody wants his or her new business to succeed, right? No one starts one with the idea of failing. Advance planning at this point of the process will pay off down the road.

In the planning stage, find out if the business requires special licenses or permits to operate legally. Also, find out if special taxes will be required to be paid. It's important to realize that all states are different; the internet is a great way to research what the business will be responsible for. Will the business need to collect or pay sales tax? In New Jersey, for instance, there is also a 'Use Tax' that most businesses are not aware they still need to pay, regardless of whether or not they pay sales tax. Additionally, some industries may have related taxes; for example, an automobile tire store in New Jersey is required to pay a tire tax of $1.50 for each old tire it discards. Find out the legal business responsibilities for the industry of the business, or one day you may hear a knock on the door, at some point down the road, from the tax official, bringing a surprise of unexpected costs and penalties.

Besides possibly setting up benefits for employees (such as a 401K) and the insurance needs (such as workman's compensation, liability, or health), it's necessary to find the right bank for the business's needs. In the business plan, detail the role of the bank for the operation of the business. Important things to consider include: What kind of bank is best for the business? Will a merchant account be required to accept credit card payments, or wire transfer capabilities for international commerce? Also, online banking and bill pay can be a time- and cost-saving way to pay expenses. Each bank is unique with how the connection between the bookkeeping software and payments to vendors is made. For example, QuickBooks has the capability, when coupled with the proper bank, to have one-step transactions where the bill to be paid gets entered, then online instructions get sent to the bank to either cut and mail a check or use ACH – which is an online, bank-to-bank payment. Sometimes there is a monthly cost. Online bill pay alone, on the other hand, may be free of charge. Do a simple cost-benefit-analysis to see if this would save money! If the business expects to write 30 checks per month, this would translate to writing 360 checks per year. The cost of a stamp, in 2012, is 45 cents, which indicates that the postage would be $162/year. There is also a cost for purchasing checks and envelopes, as well as time to process handwritten or printed checks. If the bank charges, for instance, $12 per month for you to have a direct connection from the accounting software, this would cost $144/year, but sometimes it is free. What if the business processes 80 checks a month? The savings would be greater. The more bills paid in a month, the greater the savings to perform bill paying online, resulting in a positive outcome financially. The payments can always be processed through online bill pay, and then entered separately into the accounting software, in a two-step process to save the mailing costs. Time is money, though, and if the business writes a lot of checks, the monthly cost for the service might be worthwhile. Also, consider that this may save money in the future if the business utilizes online banking for 10 or 20 years of the life of the business. Meeting with a few bank representatives will help to learn the available services and fees. If the business will have a loan and credit or debit card through the bank, keeping all the banking needs consolidated in one bank will be less confusing and may save on fees.

When a bank is not suiting the business's needs, it might be a pain to switch banks down the road. By that time, there may be several accounts, automatic deductions or deposits, credit lines, merchant accounts, etc. Having a bookkeeper to transition a bank change will save the business owner some headaches! However, taking the time to do the research and find the right bank for the business needs while in the planning stage is advisable.

For those business owners who choose to do their own bookkeeping for the business, set aside time in each week or day to input the invoicing, expenses, and income while it is still fresh in one's memory. Catching up on the bookkeeping when the income tax filing date is approaching after not doing it for a year will cause the business owner or manager stress; or, it could cause the business owner to require hiring a bookkeeper to do the inputting or pay late filing fees. Finding a good CPA is advisable. CPAs, as well as bookkeepers, can advise which expenses will need to be recorded. Setting up a good filing system is important in case several years down the road the tax official, requests the business to produce evidence for what was stated in its financial records. A scanner is a great office gadget that enables one to keep records without all the paper fuss. When companies get audited, they might have to pay costly for copies of banking information after the bank had archived electronic files after 6 or 12 months. The chances may be slim that a business will ever have to live this experience. However, without the gift of seeing into the future, one will never know what to expect... down the road. So, it is better to be prepared.

Security of the financial data is always something to be concerned with, regardless of whether the venture is a new business startup or an ongoing business. If the computer housing the bookkeeping data is used by (or available to) employees, then certainly institute a password to keep them out of the business's financial information. It is none of their concern how much money the business or the owner(s) make, or what is owed, etc. Even the most trustworthy employees can snoop, or if the relationship becomes sour at some point, their knowledge can be poison to the business!

Paper files, such as bank and credit card statements, customer credit card numbers, payroll or 401k records, and checkbooks, should always be stored in a locking file cabinet or office. Additionally, signed W-4's or W-9's need to be kept on file and no one should be privy to social security numbers except the owner, bookkeeper, and the CPA. It is a business owner's responsibility to prevent identity theft of the employees, customers, and the owner's equity. The CPA will advise how long documents should be kept.

Another element of financial security regards website security and backups. If the business does e-commerce, make sure the website is a secure site in order to sell products and receive payments. Backing up the bookkeeping files is important and needs to be accomplished either weekly or monthly by copying the files to a portable system that can be taken home or in one's briefcase; that way, in event of a fire or flood, years of records don't get destroyed. It might be difficult or impossible to replicate the data. Remote file storage is a great way to ensure the safety of the financial data. For business startups, include the costs for remote storage in the business plan. Back up the data often in case of emergency. Just like brushing one's teeth, it's better to get in the routine of doing it.

A common mistake that people unknowingly commit is thinking they can undertake the payroll function by writing a check out or paying cash to an employee as a wage. Find out what is required to have employees and make sure everything is done legally. Ignorance is not an excuse and rarely can one find a sympathetic IRS or State Department of Labor representative. Most often, there are reasonable representatives that want to see the business continue to operate and are willing to work out payment plans. Recently, a prospective client called saying a NJ Department of Labor representative knocked on the door of the business and asked to see its NJ 927 and WR 30 quarterly reports. The business owner was not filing this information as he could have easily, online. The bookkeeper needs obtained power of attorney with the state on behalf of the business and the resulting action was to file 6 years of quarterly reports, having to re-construct the data going backwards since he kept no records. The penalties, interest and unpaid tax were substantial and luckily, he was able to obtain a payment plan, otherwise, this might have resulted in closing his business or worse yet, going to jail!

When hiring a bookkeeper, find out if he or she is proficient at payroll if the business will be paying employees. Alternatively, a reputable payroll service can be an excellent solution, as it is not very costly and it usually has up-to-the-minute tax percentages and changes. These services also do all the tax filings. Oftentimes, the 'big' payroll companies are not great with customer relations (there may be 3 different people handling the account) and tend to nickel and dime for their services. On the other hand, a small company might not be experienced enough; therefore, a middle-sized company might be a good option to look into. Ask fellow business owners or friends which payroll service they use, whether there were ever any problems, what their good points are, etc. Make sure the payroll company supplies copies of the tax filings, be it monthly, quarterly, or yearly. They should relinquish the company 'pin' to get into the online reporting screen for the company in case the owners should ever want to check it themselves.

Payroll and 401K accounts also need periodic (or at least yearly) reconciliations. A call came in to update the bookkeeping for a business owner that got too busy operating the business. He was 10 months behind and he was preparing to file his income tax return for the previous year. A year end reconciliation was performed on the payroll account and it came to light he overpaid $7500 to one of the 'big' payroll companies on the year's payroll of $96,000! He was really happy that it only cost him $80 to pay a capable bookkeeper to do the leg work, they netted $7420 and his wife said she was really happy that she hired one. The bookkeeper does their maintenance now. The wife and the kids see Dad a lot more and they have peace of mind that all is being recorded legally and efficiently.

Reconciling bank and credit card statements is not always a popular function that business owners look forward to performing. It is necessary to reconcile these accounts in order to have accurate financial statements. There may be a line of credit to be utilized for automatic overdraft protection of an operating account. For those who do their own bookkeeping, they might consider hiring a bookkeeper to do these types of functions while the owner or manager may be capable of doing the invoicing, bank deposits, bill paying, etc. If the business accepts credit card payments, the merchant account needs to be observed for error and accuracy as well. While doing a clean- up of the bookkeeping for a business that sold a few different retail items via e-commerce, the author of this chapter discovered a major defect in their process. The business sold about 40 items per day through a service similar to Pay Pal. They would ship the product the next day and sometimes the customer's payment would have not gone through, for whatever reason, and the customer got the item free of charge. When scrutinized, the loss amounted to about 6% of their sales income. It may not seem like a lot of loss, but it still lowered the profit margin.

Does the company sell retail and keep inventory? There will need to be an efficient system for recording COGS (cost of goods sold) purchases and sales, decreasing the inventory. The initial setup needs to be carefully mapped, including the numbering system for the items for sale. Will items be sold in a set? If so, manual adjustments may need to be recorded. If the program to keep track of inventory is not part of the bookkeeping program, then there needs to be a way to record inventory 'in' and 'out' so COGS (cost of goods sold) is accurate. Otherwise, financial statements may be over or understated. If the business sells retail via e-commerce and has customer payments recorded though a venue like PayPal, often times the data needs to be manually entered into the bookkeeping program. To facilitate this necessity, some of the e-commerce merchants offer the sales to be converted into Excel to be able to total items. The totals can be manually entered into the accounting program such as QuickBooks. Unfortunately, QuickBooks is not efficient at bringing Excel data back into the software. There is software that can connect the 2 systems (the e-commerce account to the bookkeeping software), but it expensive and finding a perfect one to coincide with the particular business might be a challenge. Consider these added costs in the business plan so there are little surprises down the road. Regardless of how the inventory is recorded, it is important to make a count (at least yearly) to make sure there was no shrinkage that went unrecorded. Adjustments should be made periodically to avoid over or under statements of inventory items. Otherwise, you may have a customer purchase items that do not exist in the inventory.

How does one hire an excellent bookkeeper? There are many things to look for, and it's important to not simply hire the first person interviewed. It is like finding a good doctor. The goal is to find someone who is competent, trustworthy, and available; returns phone calls; is a good value for the money; and, above all, has a good connection with the business owner or management personnel. Communication is very important between the owners, the CPA, and the bookkeeper. A bookkeeper should be able to take direction from a CPA without letting his or her ego get in the way. Sometimes operations need to be tweaked between how a bookkeeper records entries and how the CPA requires the data for income tax reporting.

Additionally, a prospective bookkeeper should have a Bachelor's degree that ensures he or she was trained to follow GAAP (Generally Accepted Accounting Principles). Unlike a CPA, there is no mandatory certificate that is required to be a bookkeeper. Someone who has a BS in Accounting will be trained on how a General Ledger is maintained by recording debits, credits, reading and interpreting financial statements, etc. Having certificates for online programs or organizations does not necessarily indicate they know what they are doing. Make sure the person hired is trained to perform a bookkeeper's duty.

When it comes to bookkeeping, experience speaks volumes. On the interview, ask what type of work the bookkeeper has performed and with which industry and programs he or she is familiar. Another important aspect of experience is whether or not the bookkeeper is proficient in tax filings, reconciliations, and processing 1099 information for sub-contractors, which is a huge reason the IRS comes to look for those not complying with the laws. Certain industries frequently use subcontractors, and a bookkeeper should be able to take care of the required duties; it is not something that only your CPA can do. CPAs tend to charge more (between 2 and 3 times the cost) for their 'in-house' bookkeeper to do tasks a hired bookkeeper should be able to perform, such as printing 1099's and filing the required transmittals to the IRS and state.

Does this prospective bookkeeper work with General Ledger accounts, Trial Balances and Accounts Receivable aging found in larger sized businesses? Can they do Journal entries for adjustments and set up routine transactions to save time?

Are they familiar with whatever specialty filings you need to do for your business as detailed earlier in the examples about tire or use tax? How about their ability to use online banking services?

How available is the prospective bookkeeper and do their fees compare to others? Do they have liability insurance and what does it cover?

Ask for 6 references and call at least 3 of them. Don't forget, this bookkeeper might have access and passwords to bank accounts, credit card accounts, payroll, 401K, tax accounts, and keys to the building.

Assess with the findings and intuition, and decide if this person has a high level of integrity and confidentiality. If a current bookkeeper gives privy information to employees or customers, he or she is acting inappropriately. Get a new bookkeeper.

Once you hire the bookkeeper, establish the agreed upon duties. The prospective bookkeeper may ask new clients to sign an agreement that details the duties, fees, and payment arrangements, as well as liability and time commitment. This is not uncommon.

Additional necessary abilities for prospective bookkeepers include being able to interpret financial statements. A P&L statement (Profit and Loss), Balance Sheet, Statement of Cash Flows and Owner's

Equity are reports that indicate the financial worthiness of a business. They will show signs of illness, and problems should be addressed in a timely fashion. A competent bookkeeper should be able to point out signs of trouble.

It wouldn't hurt if the business owner took the time to educate oneself on how to read some of these statements. The bookkeeper or CPA can help with questions and answers, and observing reports either monthly or quarterly is recommended. Don't wait until the end of the year statement to find out there was little or no net income because of something such as the overhead costs being too high. In a small business, too many unnecessary 'meals and entertainment' and 'personal' expenses being charged to the business accounts will affect the profitability, in addition to being a dishonest way to operate.

Businesses need to make money and show a profit. Is that not why people go into business in the first place? At a point in the future, the owners may wish to apply for a loan to grow the business. Or, maybe they wish to sell the business after a few years of building a clientele. Showing a low net income, profit margin, or owner's equity affects to the value of the business and this would result in negative indicators. Be aware that what might be done today could have an adverse financial impact down the road.

If a business is living hand-to-mouth and barely keeping its head above water, address the problem areas and stop the bleeding. Finding the right bookkeeper might be the key to staying alive. *Don't be too proud to seek help!* There may be family members, friends, or neighbors that have had businesses that have either succeeded or failed. They may be a good source of business operating knowledge and can assist with advice as concerns arise provided they can be trusted with confidentiality. Also, a great (and sometimes free) resource is networking groups or the Chamber of Commerce in the community and this may be a good, local way to find business associates – like a CPA, payroll company or bookkeeper. The business owner's time might be more efficiently spent making the money and doing what he or she does best. Hire a bookkeeper to perform what management is neither capable of, or has the time for. It could save time, money, and stress in the long run. Most importantly, educate one's self to be a successful business owner and retire a happy and wealthy person, thanks to savvy business prowess!

Chapter 36

Getting Your Business to Survive Tough Economies

By Neil Pinkman

The things you need to do to survive tough times are the same things you should be doing not only in good economies, but all the time. However, when times are tough many business owners want a quick fix, and to take shortcuts, rather than do what should be done all the time.

You need to develop a strategic plan, not a business plan. Nine out of ten small business owners do not have a strategic plan. Most people see having a small business as the equity for their retirement. Unfortunately, only two to ten percent of businesses are actually set up to be sold. One of the most critical elements is to have a business coach. All of the most successful businesses utilize business coaches and a strategic plan, revisited frequently. A successful business is defined as one that operates profitably without the owner working in the business.

Also, you need to develop a successful vision for the next 10-15 years. Then the business owner needs to do an internal appraisal and external assessment that capture key assumptions – these, combined with the vision, equal the mission. The mission statement includes how many people, how many locations, etc. Where do you want to be 24-36 months down the road, in detail? From that you will derive critical goal categories. These should be five-eight areas that must be addressed in order to meet the mission that drives to vision.

Examples of the five categories include new product development, physical location, marketing, staff, and sales. They need to meet sufficiency and necessity tests.

Once you have five-eight critical goal categories, then come up with specific goals for each category. Each category may have a dozen or more specific goals. Then each goal is broken down to include possible obstacles, then possible solutions, then specific action steps. These steps drive the budgets, the market plan and sales plan. Budget can also be broken down per category; this is normally done with a financial planner and CPA.

Regardless of where the business is, whether it is currently profitable or struggling and teetering on the edge of bankruptcy, it is critical to go through each of the above steps; the process forces you to see opportunities that are right in front of you all the time that you normally might not otherwise recognize.

The most common mistake being made in these very difficult economic times is that people are not re-investing in themselves and their business. They just put their head in the sand, which will result in businesses being forced to fold/file bankruptcy.

MOST COMMON PATH TO FAILURE

The biggest misconception in measuring the success of a business is that a successful business must have a lot of employees and be a large company. The real measure of a successful company is how much money the owner puts into his "pocket" at the end of each year, a.k.a. the most profitable with the least outlay for overhead.

Regardless of how bad times are, in every industry there is someone doing well and making a lot of money – this can be YOUR business if YOU have an effective strategic plan that you create and follow.

Examples of companies that have re-invested in themselves:

Example 1

>Type of company: construction-residential home remodeling

>Time frame starting with business coach: Oct/Nov 2008 to current.

>Age of company at start: five years

At the start, this company's sales had plateaued, and the owner was concerned that sales would dangerously decline due to the economy and how others in the industry were performing. The owner hired a business coach, created and followed a strategic plan, and identified new market segments which resulted in a growth rate of 30% per year in the last two years (during the recession of 2008-2010). During those two years, many others in the same construction industry were forced to file bankruptcy or lay off many of their employees. These were deviating economic times for all the real estate and construction related industries.

Example 2

>Type of company: graphic design company (brochure and web design)

>Time frame starting with business coach: Sept/Oct 2009

>Age of company at start: seven years

The decision to hire a business coach was made because the sole owner hired only freelance workers who desired growth. The primary step that was implemented was developing and following the strategic plan; the result was that in six months, the gross sales doubled, and the owner hired a full time project manager.

Example 3

Type of company: holistic wellness center

Time frame starting with business coach: 2002–2004

Age of company at start: one year

Unfortunately a common mistake of startup businesses is that they get caught up in the excitement of the fun details of starting the business, such as the business name, logo, and marketing, but fail to develop a strategy first. It is the strategy that defines who those loyal customers are whom you are trying to attract and retain. Until you have done the strategy and know who your target market is, you do not know who you are marketing to. This inevitably wastes much of the startup cash flow, which is the reason for the famous ratio that 80% of businesses fail in the first five years.

When they first hired their business coach they had only 40 appointments per week. After one year, they doubled the square footage of the business location, tripled their staff, and grew to more than 120 appointments a week by simply creating, executing and closely following their strategic plan.

There has been much conversation from the current administration to address these issues. In fact, health reform has been on the forefront and has been a priority for President Obama. Unfortunately, there has been much confusion and frustration in this regard. At this point in time the small business owner has not witnessed any relief.

These contributing factors do not present for a very positive forecast for the small business owner in New Jersey, as well as in many other states. The stress and anxiety levels are increasing rapidly, causing a ripple effect which will inevitably cause hardship for not just the small business owners and their employees but, on a large scale, the economy as a whole. Furthermore, in many instances the end result will be that many small business owners will be forced to "fold their tents" and shut their doors, causing additional unemployment.

Chapter 37

Create a "Get Off Your A$$" Mindset

By Sean Carroll

To be a successful entrepreneur, you simply can't wait for things to happen. You need to MAKE them happen. If you're the type of person that likes to take charge, create opportunity, or head up a project, there's a good chance you already have an entrepreneurial advantage.

I call this having a "Get Off Your A$$" mindset.

It is a belief system that says: "I am in control of my own destiny. I believe my success is directly dependent upon my own efforts, abilities, planning, and ability to be resourceful. Circumstances do NOT define me. I have choices in how I respond to things. I am not a victim. I create my own economy, and don't wait for things to change before I create opportunity."

Having a Get Off Your A$$ mindset will not make you invincible, but it will give you a tremendous competitive advantage, because believe it or not, there are millions of people who still believe that they are not successful because of someone or something else. As soon as you take responsibility for your own actions and your own success or failure, you are considerably ahead of most of your competition.

But how do you use this mindset in your everyday operations and decisions as an entrepreneur? Well, the answer is simple. You just DO. It sounds simple, and it is. To help you in this process, I have outlined the seven traits I believe you need to reinforce this decision you've made to Get Off Your A$$ and get to work!

1. Desire

You have to want this. You have to WANT to get off your A$$. That sounds trivial, but I have encountered many "would be" entrepreneurs who actually told me they really weren't motivated. I can tell you from experience that if you don't want entrepreneurial success badly enough, I can promise you that you will not last. There are too many emotional ups and downs to sustain.

You have to want this more than you've ever wanted anything in your life. Remember, if it were easy, everyone would do it. The best way I know how to ensure that you want this badly, is to have a very clear reason WHY this has to succeed. Make it a must.

Desire is more than just saying "I want success". It's more than just hoping for the best. It is a burning feeling in your gut that you can't ignore. It's the feeling you get when you first wake up, that you can't wait to get to work because you just want to achieve greatness more than anything else.

Truly successful entrepreneurs have a strong desire to fulfill their purpose or their mission. It's more than just wanting financial success. It's believing in what you are doing, and believing in the reasons why you want to share this gift with the world. Entrepreneurs who are lacking in desire can make lots of money in the short term, but eventually the burnout sets in. There are lots of long days, lots of rejection, and lots of disappointment. Desire is what allows you to experience those moments as minor setbacks, instead of crushing blows. When you want it badly enough, you will simply dust yourself off and get back in the game.

2. **Passion**

This word gets thrown around a lot. Lots of people say they are passionate about what they do. What does this actually mean?

At first glance, it may seem like passion and desire are the same thing, but in fact they are quite different. Desire has to do with being hungry. Passion is about getting excited!

In order to Get Off Your A$$ and make a difference, you just have to be excited about what you're doing. If you're not, please do yourself a favor and pick something else. You're only setting yourself up for problems later on. Trust me, I know.

If you aren't excited about what you're building or what you're selling, how can you expect the marketplace to get excited about buying it? Passion is the one thing you can't fake. People can sense whether you are genuinely excited about what you're doing, or whether you're putting on a show. Any decent actor can put on a show. Only a passionate entrepreneur can build a lasting profitable business.

You may be thinking that I am suggesting that you have to become Tony Robbins and learn to talk loud, fast, and persuasively as he does at his seminars. That's not what I am saying at all. Passion looks different for everyone.

If you're a computer programmer for example, I doubt you will be jumping up and down and shouting as you're writing HTML code for your website. You might, however, be listening to your favorite music while you're doing it, and not even noticing that six hours just went by because you were so engaged in what you are doing.

For some, passion shows up in energized presentations. For others, it can be tears or laughter. It all depends on you. All that matters is that however you show your passion, it needs to be real, and it needs to be intense.

Part of your job as a business owner is to communicate with others about the benefits of your product or service. Would you buy from someone who was indifferent about their company? Or would you buy from the person who was clearly excited, and as a result, got you excited too? I know which one I would choose every time!

3. **Focus**

This is a tough one for entrepreneurs to get. We tend to be victims of what I've heard called "shiny object syndrome". We have a tendency to not only Get Off Our A$$es, but we fly at 150 miles per hour, bouncing off tasks like a ping pong ball, and then crashing down to earth with all of the debris we created around us.

The most successful entrepreneurs combine all the elements of desire, passion, and our third skill, which is focus.

Being focused on one thing at a time enables you to experience extraordinary progress in that area. It is similar to what happens when you take a magnifying glass and harness the rays of the sun onto a piece of paper. By itself, the sun can warm a very large area rather evenly, but when you focus the sun's rays using that magnifying glass, you can burn a hole through a sheet of paper, or even start a fire.

The only difference between a laser and a the light from your desk lamp is the intensity and the focus. When someone says they are "laser focused", they mean they are harnessing all of their energy, desire, and passion towards one goal. That's how you get results.

I can hear some of you saying: "But Sean, isn't multi-tasking part of being a good entrepreneur?" The answer is yes, and no. Let's face it, sometimes we need to be spinning a few plates and working on a few things at a time. However on the really important things, we MUST have focus, or we'll never see the kind of results that we really want.

In my "Get Off Your A$$ Academy" training course, I help

entrepreneurs become laser focused, so they can get more done, in less time, with better results. By allowing too many things to occupy our time and attention, we are actually adding more time to each project. It's much better to focus, and do one job well, than to do five jobs in a mediocre fashion.

4. **Integrity**

    Integrity simply means doing what you say you're going to do. There was a time in business where a handshake actually was enough to secure a multi-million dollar transaction. In some circles, that may still be the case, but more often than not, there needs to be endless paper trails, attorneys, compliance officers and regulations because less and less people actually do what they say they are going to do.

    Having integrity means not only being honest, but following through. If you attend a networking meeting and tell someone you are going to forward them a copy of an article that might help their business, DO IT! Go back to your office and immediately take care of it, or at least schedule a time when you will do it in the next 24 hours.

    If you offered someone an introduction to a person in your network, make sure you deliver on what you promised. There is a principle I live by which is "under promise, and over deliver". This means that I really try not to promise anything that I feel like I can't deliver. Or, I promise it at a time or at a level that I am confident I can comply with, but then exceed that level because I was more conservative in my promise.

    Wouldn't you rather under promise and over deliver than do what many people do instead? How do you feel when someone OVER promises and then UNDER delivers? I'll bet it has an effect on your level of trust or respect for that person. It may not sabotage the relationship the first time, but I guarantee it has an effect.

    Another key component of integrity is showing up on time. It seems our society has little respect for appointment times anymore. Whether it's a doctor's office, a court appointment, or even a Broadway show, it seems that all times are approximate.

I understand that sometimes stuff happens and you're going to be late. That's normal. But instead of just having the standard that it's OK to be late, how about having the standard that the only acceptable outcome is to be there on time.

I get annoyed with myself when I'm late. I hope you do too. If you don't have this standard, I suggest changing your thinking. If you can't show up on time for an appointment, give me one good reason why I should trust you when buying your product or service. Sorry. . . there isn't one. I feel that strongly about it. I believe the little things matter, and in this case, the little thing of showing up on time has proven to be nearly 100% accurate when I am evaluating someone's level of service.

5. **Perseverance:**

Too many people give up when something gets hard.

I learned a saying from one of my early mentors. He told me "Don't give up before the miracle happens." In other words, you just never know when all the hard work is going to pay off, and it would be a real shame to quit right before the tipping point.

One of the world's most famous motivational speakers, Zig Ziglar, used to illustrate this beautifully with his Prime The Pump presentation. He showed audiences how you needed to prime a water pump to get water from a well. He would vigorously move the pump up and down for several minutes, long before any water would come out.

Imagine, he said, that the water that's on its way up the well, is the payoff for all of your hard work until this point. You could be doing all this heavy work, and the water is on the way up towards the spout. Once the water comes through the spout, you don't need to pump as aggressively. You just keep pumping steadily, and the water continues to flow.

But, if you quit pumping too soon, or don't pump hard enough, you will not get to experience the rewards of the hard work.

How often have you quit something, when the water was just about to come through the spout? Don't let that happen.
A successful entrepreneur needs to push through the negative thoughts, and will not make a decision that will affect their entire business based on the emotion of the day.

Even when it hurts, or is uncomfortable, the successful business owner will keep pushing through those moments, because he/she knows, the water will appear.

No one said that being an entrepreneur was easy. If it were easy, everyone would do it. The rewards are worth it, but if you're not willing to show up consistently through the difficult times, and push through those moments of fear and uncertainty, you're better off working for someone else. Really. I'm being that honest with you, because nothing is more true.

6. **Courage (Guts)**

Sometimes, you're going to have to do something that you're afraid to do. There will be rejection. There will be people who tell you that you're crazy. There will be times when you need to invest in your business, instead of spending money on personal things. There will be times that you have to negotiate with someone that has more experience, or more education. Embrace these moments!

A successful entrepreneur has guts. Notice I didn't say you won't be afraid. I said you'd be afraid, and then do the action anyway. In my audio course, ***The Get Off Your A$$ Academy***, I help entrepreneurs to use fear as an asset, instead of a liability.

Never let fear alone be the reason you don't move forward on something. Use the fear as a means to pull you towards right action, instead of wasting your energy trying to fight the fear. By fighting, you are only giving fear exactly what it wants. Take that same energy, and surge ahead. Call that prospect. Raise your price. Turn down that offer. Do the right thing, no matter how afraid you are.

A successful entrepreneur should also have the guts to take a position on something. Have an opinion! Don't try to be all things to all people. Our world needs leaders, not people who will bend and move with whatever winds are blowing that day. When you are making a presentation, and someone takes a shot at your idea, stick up for yourself. Come prepared with facts to substantiate your position, but don't just back down and agree because you're afraid.

You don't want to be seen as arrogant, but you do want confidence. Arrogance is the belief that you are right, no matter what the set of facts are. Confidence is KNOWING you are right, because you have the facts and the experience to back up your claim.

While someone can disagree with you, no one can argue with your experience. It's your story! They can't dispute the facts about the things you've experienced. Take your position, and support it passionately!

7. **Discipline**

This word gets a bad reputation. When some people hear the word discipline, they think about punishment. That's not what I'm talking about. I'm talking about the ability to put off immediate gratification, for something that's going to help your business in the long term.

For example, if you and your friend both got a sizable income tax refund check, and your friend suggested you go out to an expensive meal in the city, a disciplined entrepreneur would see that money as a potential investment in the business.

I'm not saying you need to deprive yourself of anything fun. I'm saying you need to have your priorities straight, and then act on those priorities properly.

It's not just about money either. In fact, time is wasted much more than money ever will be. Time is the one thing you can never get back once it's gone. You can't go to the store and buy more, and you can't borrow it from someone else. Once it's gone, it's gone.

Having discipline means that just because you don't have a boss telling you to report to work from 9 to 5, you've set your own standard that you will be working full time during those hours. You won't go grocery shopping. You won't go to the barber or the nail salon. You will work. Whatever you need to do that day to help your business during those hours, you will do it.

I hear what you might be thinking. "But one of the reasons I want to be my own boss is so I can have flexibility with my schedule." I understand. I feel that way, too. All I am saying is that you need to decide when you are working and when you're not. There is no place for halfhearted work.

The same thing applies for your family or personal time. If you're on a date with your significant other, I strongly suggest you do NOT check your email during dinner. Work hard when you're working, but when it's time to shut off the business for a few hours, make sure you have the discipline to do that.

It's often not easy. I get it. I understand.

What I've learned, though, is that truly successful people are willing to do things that average people are not. The average person would have ice cream for dessert two-four times per week. The athlete would say "The temporary pleasure of that ice cream is not worth the longer term effects."

Think the same way about your business. Be willing to put off the instant gratification, so you can do the things that are going to be best for your business in the long run.

I commend you for taking the leap and deciding to start your own business and become an entrepreneur. That alone takes guts. I wish you nothing but success along the journey, and am excited for you, because I know how this experience will shape you into an even more amazing person than you already are.

If something I said offended you, Good. That means I hit a nerve close to home. If I inspired you. Good. That means you got encouragement that reinforced your belief that you can succeed as an entrepreneur.

I love working with entrepreneurs. I love people with guts, and a desire to constantly grow. I'm always looking to help people who are hungry. If you are ready to take this to the next level, I highly recommend checking out my Get Off Your A$$ Academy, which is designed to help entrepreneurs go to the next level.

I take people like you who are already talented, experienced, and smart, and help them accomplish more, in less time. I help people like you become more influential and more persuasive when you communicate. I show you how to build powerful and profitable networks, and make the most of every opportunity to add people to your network. Most importantly, I help you gain control of that beast known as fear, and use it as one of your greatest assets.

Make it a great life!

Chapter 38

Psychological Tips for the Entrepreneur to Stay the Course Through Tough Times

By Rich Dowling, MA, LPC, MAC

You're living your dream as a successful business owner, the economy takes a down turn, and business drops off. What to do? How can you get through without "losing your mind" and maybe your dream!

Tip #1. Unconditional Acceptance of Self, Others, and the World (U.A.S.O.W.)

First things first. Step back, take a deep breath, and accept that you do not have control over the state of the economy, but you do have control over how you react. Unconditional Acceptance of Reality (UAoR) can save you from some serious emotional distress and distraction from the job at hand, or in this case, saving your business! UAoR does not mean a given person, place, or thing is "good," "right," or "fair." It simply means seeing it as it is and deciding how you can best deal with it rather than "demanding" it be something different than it really is. Seeing things as they really are and not as you think they "should" be puts you on the path to emotional stability, enabling you to not only feel comfortable emotionally but also to think and function more to your ability. Things may be "bad" at times, but why make them seem worse than they really are? The good news is you do have control over how you react to a given situation through your ability to Think and Reason. In fact, THINKING is the one thing you do have most control over in this life and it can be your best asset or worst liability depending on how you utilize it, as Tip #2 and Tip #3 demonstrate.

Tip #2. It's All in How You See It!!! Semantics' Role in Whether You Sink or Swim!

Do you see a given situation as a "Crisis" or a "Challenge"? The words we choose to use and how we understand them can make a dramatic difference in how we react to a given situation. For many, the belief that they are facing a "crisis" can lead to "awfulizing" a situation, making it seem worse than it really is. This is the stuff emotional dis-stress (i.e., depression, anxiety, anger, guilt, and shame) is made of. On the other hand, thinking of a situation as a "challenge" can offer hope, opportunity, and even "eu-stress". Never heard of "eu-stress"? You are not alone, most haven't, but most have experienced it. It's the high end of the stress continuum with calm and relaxed in the middle. It's the type of stress those who say they work better under pressure experience. You know, the adrenaline pumping, take charge, get it done types.

The reality is that humans generally feel and behave the way they think, and can change the way they feel and behave by changing their thinking, provided they are motivated, acquire personally meaningful information, and are determined and persistent in their efforts.

If you're not so sure about this, read Tip #3 and practice the ABCs.

Tip #3. ABCs of REBT for Feeling and Behaving More the Way You Prefer

"People generally feel and behave the way they think," ancient philosopher Epictetus noted 2000 years ago. Modern day psychologist Albert Ellis (www.albertellis.org) developed the ABC formula around this idea to help people evaluate and enhance their emotions and behaviors. Maintaining emotional comfort and stability during a "crisis" can be very helpful. It seems appropriate at this point to reference Rudyard Kipling's "If you can keep your head when all about you are losing theirs..." For many, this may seem easier said than done, but it can be as "simple" as learning and practicing the ABCs of REBT (Rational Emotive Behavior Therapy, www.rebt.org).

Don't let the "therapy" reference turn you off; this is a sound philosophical and educational model for taking charge of your feelings and behavior in general. It's the way humans function, put in an easily workable formula. As a basic tutorial let me offer this:

A = Activating event: any person, place, or thing we experience

B = Belief: our beliefs about A generally determine

C = Consequences: feelings and behaviors.

Many people mistakenly believe it's the "A" that will determine how they feel and behave, i.e., "He made me mad." In other words, they believe they have no choice in how they feel or behave given certain circumstances. This is so NOT TRUE, and is the basis for much of the emotional upset and counterproductive behavior humans experience! The object of "doing" an ABC is to "document" and evaluate the emotional and/or behavioral experience, and then using two additional letters of the alphabet:

D = Dispute: question the validity of your belief, e.g., "The economy is terrible, business stinks, it's terrible, I can't stand it and I feel depressed, I need a drink." "Is what I am telling myself true, reasonable, rational? No, just because the economy takes a downturn doesn't mean I have to feel 'stressed out,' give up hope or drink myself silly." You identify, question, dispute the iBs=Irrational Beliefs, exchange them for rBs=Rational Beliefs, experiencing the:

E = Effect of enhanced emotional comfort and productive behaviors. Sound like a lot of psychobabble? Well, putting it to practice will demonstrate the benefit, so give it a try and see for yourself! That's right, "Change Your Thinking, Enhance Your Life"!™, including the possibility of enhancing your business. For a more in depth explanation of the ABCs of REBT, visit www.rebt.org or www.albertellis.org.

Tip #4. Time to do a (CBA) Cost Benefit Analysis

Is it time to go out of, or time to stay in, business? This is the question.

Now that you have your emotions in check, and you're not drowning your sorrows in whiskey, beer, or wine, it's time to do a "CBA," Cost Benefit Analysis. How motivated are you to tough out the tough times? How likely is it the business will survive? How motivated are you to give it a try? The CBA is not only a common business tool, as you are probably aware, but is commonly used by humans on a daily basis, whether consciously or not, to evaluate and decide the value and benefit of any number of things in one's life. So let's get busy with analysis, analysis.

The basic CBA is set out like this: four columns, or four quadrants.

Make a comprehensive list of:

1. the known or possible benefits or rewards of staying in business.
2. the known or possible costs or risks of staying in business
3. the known or possible benefits or rewards of closing the business
4. the known or possible costs or risks of closing the business.

Specifying the short and long term of each item is suggested.

Think long and hard, see every possibility, ask for HELP!

The CBA can offer clarity as to the reality of the situation, making a decision easier and hopefully less painful. Whether the business is a go or not the 5th Tip is one I encourage you to enhance and practice on a regular basis if for no other reason than "just for the FUN of it!"

Tip #5. SMILE and LAUGH: Finding Humor Even in "The Worst of Times!"

This is a lesson I learned from my father, one I greatly appreciate and thank him for. Smiling and laughing can make the "worst" seem less so, and more manageable as well.

What's that you say, can't see anything funny about the situation? How about some self-deprecating humor to start, that is laughing at yourself for making things seem worse than they really are and for leaving yourself feeling worse than is necessary?

The CBA you did has hopefully given a renewed degree of motivation to forge ahead, so now there is nothing stopping you from looking for ways to grow your business even in this tough time, is there? So get to it! Brainstorm, brainstorm, brainstorm. Maybe it's time to tighten your business's belt, or there may be a niche market you have overlooked, for example. Now that you have your "head screwed on right," emotionally speaking, and you are behaving like the good business person you are, this may be the time to review other chapters in this book and other note resources for the many good suggestions offered!

Chapter 39

Should You Throw In The Towel? Evaluate Current Status, Growth History, and Growth Potential

By Donna Price

Operating a business is no easy task. I have always relied on three principles or values: commitment, perseverance, and risk. It takes all of these to make it in business. If you are considering going into business and you don't have these traits or characteristics, you should throw in the towel before you start because these are essential. Once you are in business, you have to keep going back to these.

A long time ago I learned about commitment when I was rock climbing. I was high off the ground. You know stories grow as you tell them and at one point in this story I was hundreds of feet off the ground but really probably about 30 feet off the ground. High enough!! I was stuck. I could feel the next place for my foot but it was just out of reach. I could see the hand hold but I couldn't reach it. Precariously perched on the side of the mountain, I searched for alternatives. My belayer (the person holding my rope/my life) was patient with me. After I had exhausted all of the possibilities and didn't find an alternative he said "you have to commit to the move, you just have to go for it." He meant I had to let go of the safety of my perch and reach out, risk, and make a commitment to making it to the next hold. I took a deep breath and did it. I made the move and I learned a lesson.

In my business, I have used that lesson over and over. There are many metaphors there: taking a risk, staying focused on my path, and commitment. When I have questioned my business, I go back to the rocks of Joshua Tree National Monument and remember that it takes total commitment to be successful in business, and that I have to "commit to the move."

Next is perseverance. I learned this lesson biking across the country from Maine to Oregon. Now that in itself takes some perseverance, but the real lesson came in Wyoming in the Big Horn Mountains. We had to cross the Rocky Mountains somewhere and the Big Horns looked like the best option. The climb was 30+ miles long. For me, that means I am biking between three and six miles per hour for a very long time. There I learned that no matter how slow I was going, I had to keep pushing that pedal to make it to the top of the mountain. There are times when in business it feels like a BIG mountain climb. Some days the mountain is not as steep and the climb isn't as long, and some days it is a very long climb. But I also know that it is perseverance that keeps me moving my business forward. One of the tools that I use is an accomplishment list or journal. There are days when you are climbing that mountain or putting out fires that you just can't see what you have accomplished. An accomplishment journal helps because when you start listing all of the things that you did do, it is amazing. It can energize you and keep you moving.

Finally, there is risk. Business is risk. You are stepping out of the comfort zone of a JOB and into being an entrepreneur. Not everyone can take that risk and live with it. Sometimes the risk lasts for a long time before the payoff comes. You have to know yourself, what you can tolerate, and what your life can tolerate.

When you are in business, you are in the driver's seat, and you are making the decisions about what is acceptable.

It is vital that you are looking at your entire business. You need to have your finger on the pulse of your organization in several areas:

Vision – You need to have a clear and compelling vision that helps to energize you and draws you into the future. Be clear on what you are creating so that you don't get distracted or pulled off track.

Strategy – Create strategies to accomplish the vision. Keep your strategies in front of you and know where you are with each one. So many strategic plans get put aside and never referenced after they are created.

Money – you need to know your numbers. This is one area that I was never good at. My business did not start taking off until I put my finger on the pulse of the money. You need to know what is coming in and going out. Know the numbers. Know what it takes to make you profitable; know where you are now and how far away you are from that profitability.

Staff – Know what is going on with your staff if you have them. Know their vision and their passion. Stay in touch with what is happening on the floor. There is incredible information there.

SO WHAT DO YOU DO WHEN THE PULSE IS LOW?

This is perhaps the hardest question you will ever answer. YOU have to make the decision and you need to rely on several factors.

First, listen to your own wisdom. Many times we know what we need to do and we ignore the inner voice that is telling us. We get further down the road and, in hindsight, it is clear; then we can even acknowledge that we know. Listening to yourself and your feeling and gut is important.

You also have to be a wise business owner. That means that you have to take a look at the facts in front of you.

You've been paying attention to your business. You know its current state and you know its growth.

Evaluate: Current Status, Growth History, and Growth Potential.
What is the current status of the organization? Are you still investing money in it? Has it been three years? Five years? Can you afford to continue investing? Does that fit into your life plan? Or is it self-supporting?

What is the growth history? Has the business been growing? Adding new clients? New customers? Is that growth consistent? Is the product or service still in demand? Have you evaluated the potential growth of the product/service? Do you know your market?

If your business is struggling, have you exhausted all of your marketing strategies to bring in new customers or repeat customers?

As the business owner considering throwing in the towel, you must not leave any stone unturned. If there is a marketing strategy that you haven't tried because you are personally uncomfortable with it, now is the time to get comfortable. For instance, if you are not tech savvy and don't like being on the Internet – you have to have an Internet presence. You cannot be in business and not have an I Internet presence. You must have a social media presence.

Are there things that you can be outsourcing that will free you up to do the sales side or development side of the business? As the owner or CEO, your role is to build the business and develop the business. This may mean networking, connecting, landing new clients, new investors, new products, or services. You know what business building looks like for your business. What are your business development strategies? Do you have the time to carry them out? If not, what can you delegate in order to do that?

If you are spending your valuable time doing non-essential tasks then you need to re-order what you do so that you can do the essential and fundamental task of business development.

Make a list each day of the essential money-focused tasks and do them first. Delegate or outsource the other tasks. Many business owners have discovered the magic of outsourcing. Suddenly, you have the time to make more money. You have handed off jobs, you are paying money to have someone else do them, and you are making MORE money! How sweet is that? What can you hand off? Now is the time to figure that out.

But wait! You still have the towel in your hand, and you are still unsure whether you should hold it or throw it in. So far, you have taken a look at your business owner characteristics of commitment, perseverance, and risk taking. You have evaluated the current state of the organization and the future growth potential, you have looked at all of your marketing and sales strategies to be sure that you are doing EVERYTHING you can to bring in clients and business, and finally, you have taken a look at yourself to determine what other things you can do to grow the business and what you can outsource or delegate to free you up to do that. After taking a look at all of this and listening to your inner voice, it should be pretty clear what to do. You know what to do. The decision may be difficult, but it is yours alone.

Whatever you decide to do it is important to do it with style, with grace, and with the utmost professionalism. Do not burn bridges. Do not do anything to harm your reputation or that of your staff, your vendors, your board, or others. If you throw in the towel, make sure it is clean, that it shines brightly, and provides everyone involved the most potential for future success possible.

Chapter 40

10 Ideas for Your Next Business Startup

By Vivian C. Gaspar

Here is an opportunity to start businesses in which you can opt not just to be self-employed, but to hire others to grow your business at no or very low cost to start up.

1) Virtual Assistant by the hour or project – hire others – don't just do it yourself. Target small business owners, professionals (attorneys, CPAs, etc.), and part-time adult college students (e.g., MBA students).

2) Manage social media for professionals: Facebook, Twitter, LinkedIn, etc.

3) Evening and overnight babysitting service for second and third shift workers.

4) Portable car cleaning service. Go to office complexes and offer to detail cars while people work. Also, offer an employee benefit by marketing to small businesses to get volume and repeat customers.

5) Telemarketing Services. Offer lead generation and seminar seat-filling services (we have a cold calling "how-to" chapter in this very book).

6) Small event planning can have specific targets (e.g., help busy parents organize and plan their child's bar/bat mitzvah or Sweet 16, which is a huge undertaking for families where both parents work).

7) Packing and unpacking service for those moving. Again, this is a huge benefit for busy families who would love for someone who is reliable to help them pack up and then unpack their home for a move. Additionally, single working parents especially need this help.

8) Organize special events, such as a speed dating event or a murder–mystery night, for restaurants/catering halls to help them bring in traffic. You can charge the customers and keep a part of each attendance fee as your fee so that it is truly a "win-win" for the restaurant/catering hall.

9) Service to help elderly in their own homes. This idea is more for emergencies at night or just to help them go to the bathroom in the middle of the night. As an unlicensed care giver, you can save the elderly person's family a lot of money over a night nurse but provide valuable peace of mind.

10) Organize and throw tricky trays (Chinese/Silent Auctions) as a fund raiser for any organization and keep a portion for your fee (e.g., 35% of all monies raised). Again, another "win-win" for any organization from a hospital, school organization (such as high school sports team), or an animal shelter, etc.

All of these ideas can be done as a sole operator (by yourself) or as a service business where you hire a staff.

*Meet
Vivian C. Gaspar*

Vivian Gaspar is an author, keynote speaker, entrepreneur, and independent business owner of several businesses over the last 25 years. Ms. Gaspar is dedicated to helping her clients survive critical financial times and achieve success.

As the Chief Mortgage Modification Specialist with V. James Castiglia's legal office in New Jersey, she reached out to and worked with over 300 families to help them keep their homes from foreclosure. Ms. Gaspar has given over a hundred key note addresses on mortgage modification, foreclosure mediation, and identity theft prevention at a variety of venues. Some of these venues included The Learning Annex, Department of Labor, various township adult education classes, local libraries, and numerous civic organizations, such as Lions and Rotary clubs.

Ms. Gaspar currently assists business owners in attaining critical capital and merchant services as a representative of Senape Capital. Senape Capital provides access to emergency and small business funding and merchant services. Ms. Gaspar also provides affordable access to legal services through Legal Shield, a legal services vendor, as well as identity theft protection and restoration. Ms. Gaspar has a wealth of knowledge on managing personal and professional crises from her years of working with individuals and businesses in crisis.

Her passion is to share her deep knowledge of navigating crises with the general public through frequent network television and radio appearances in which she speaks on a variety of topics, from entrepreneurship to identity theft. Her recent books, "Stop My Crisis- Facing Life's Challenges Head On" and "Stop My Crisis- Be the 1 in 5" are part of her latest effort to empower people with the diverse information that they need to move past their current crisis into prosperity and successfully follow their dreams.

Vivian is the author of the chapter *10 Ideas for Your Next Business Startup* and co-author of the chapters *Merchant Services: Understanding the Costs and Uses to Getting New Clients*; and *Alternative Business Financing: Bridge Your Financial Gap*.

You may reach Vivian through the information below:

Vivian@VivianGaspar.com
www.StopMyCrisis.com

*Meet
Michele J.
Alexander*

Michele Jackson Alexander is the owner of two distinct businesses: *Jackson, Jackson & Jackson*, a Professional Tax, Paralegal, and Notary business and *Win A Crown*, a production company that mainstreams local talent and pageant competitions such as The Miss Pittsburgh Pageant and The Steel City Youth Talent Competition through distinct marketing initiatives. Michele's professional work experience and background includes grant writing, negotiating federal contracts, management of individual and business tax matters including preparing clients for that IRS tax audit. Michele has also operated federally-funded employment and training programs as Executive Director and CEO for Training Agencies with OIC, the Urban League, and the Broward Economic Development Corporation, a CDC. She holds a B.A. in Liberal Arts from Shaw University, Raleigh, NC. She is also certified as a Paralegal by Legal Standards and Requirements for the Commonwealth of Pennsylvania. She is an Authorized IRS E-File Provider and Tax Preparer for the IRS, Department of the Treasury.

Michele is the author of the chapter *Should I Hire an Intern?*

You may reach Michele at malexander@jacksonparalegals.com; misspittsburghpageant@gmail.com; or at 412.224.4022.

Deborah Anderson

Ms. Anderson holds a BA from Rutgers University and a Master's Degree from Fordham University. Her extensive background in marketing and sales started in high school working for various newspapers and contractors.

Upon completion of her master's degree in 1989, it was the height of the recession and the most beneficial opportunities presented themselves in marketing and sales.

After a short career in the financial industry of banking, Ms. Anderson found success in working days for a market research firm and evenings as a manager for a telemarketing company. Ms. Anderson has seen how rewarding life is owning a telemarketing/sales company. She is now in her 18th year working with sales executives and corporations ranging from AT&T to Prudential.

Deborah is the author of the chapter *Cold Calling Tips for Business Owners And Salespeople.*

You may reach Deborah at Future Waves Marketing at 732-274-9399 or by email at futwavmkt@aol.com.

*Meet
Rose Benson*

It wasn't until the middle 1990's that Rose Benson finally decided what she wanted to be when she grew up. Rose was nearing the end of a chapter in her life as a stay at home mother and about to join the throes of single parenthood.

Rose always had a dream of becoming a CPA and began taking two or three courses a semester at the County College of Morris and graduated with honors and an Associate in Science degree in 1998. Juggling the mothering of two teens, working part-time, and pursuing a Bachelor's degree at Centenary College, Rose formed a cleaning service business to afford the flexibility, decent pay, and being able to capitalize on the benefits of self-employment. She also worked with CPAs doing data entry and auditing projects.

It took Rose eight years of persistence to finally graduate from Centenary College in 2006, Magna Cum Laude, with a Bachelor of Science in Accounting. After working for CPAs and being billed out for three times her wage, she formed **Benson Bookkeeping, LLC** in 2009 and just celebrated her third anniversary! Rose has been inn accounting since 1997 and in her years in the business have proven to be diverse, challenging, and rewarding. She performs set-ups, clean-ups, maintenance, and auditing projects. Although she has a BS, she is still learning every day. Rose says, "No two clients or businesses are ever *the same*." The first two years for Rose were a struggle, which may have been due to the economic downturn for small business (her target market), but her business has grown thanks to advice from a dear friend, Liz Crystal, and a well-placed ad on Bookkeepinghelp.com and joining local networking groups. Rose has found forming friendships with fellow entrepreneurs **priceless.**

Rose prides herself on lessons learned as a child to be honest, with a high level of integrity, personable, and giving. It has molded her as an entrepreneur and contributes to her morals of being a bookkeeper.

Roses says "Long Valley, New Jersey is a wonderful place to reside. Country living, gardening, bird watching, kayaking, skiing, traveling, charity work, and socializing are pastimes that 'charge my battery.' Life is too short not to have fun."

Rose is satisfied with her persona and the clientele she has established as a bookkeeper. Achieving a CPA degree is on her "bucket list." Her children, Amy and Karl, and her family and friends have been supportive with her transition and she would not trade any of them for all the money in the world. "Life is a book with many chapters. We sometimes write our own, but with outside influences. You never know what tomorrow will bring. Be the best you can be – whether in business or in your personal life! Carpe diem!"

Rose is the author of the chapter *Efficiency Tips To Save You Stress*.

Rose may be reached at Rose@Bensonbookkeeping.com or on Linkedin at http://www.linkedin.com/in/rosebensonbookkeeping.

Meet
Jack M. Bleiberg, CPA

Jack is a practicing CPA who has a developed proficiency in guiding companies to reach their full potential through proper planning and execution and maximizing operational efficiency and controls. He also works with his clients to protect their wealth with proper tax, business exit, and estate planning. Jack has worked with all sizes of entities from small through large public companies.

Jack has been a partner at a regional CPA firm and owned and operated business systems and consulting firms. Jack has over twenty-five years of experience owning and operating small businesses. He has extensive experience across many industries.

Jack is a graduate of Lehigh University where he obtained a Bachelor's Degree in Accounting. He has been published in the CPA Journal and chaired a committee of the New Jersey Society of CPAs. Jack is currently Vice President and Executive Board Member at the Daughters of Israel Geriatric Center in West Orange, New Jersey. He is a member of the American Institute of CPAs, the New Jersey Society of CPAs, and is active with the North Essex Chamber of Commerce.

Jack is the author of the chapter *The Power and Value of Your Business Plan*.

You may reach Jack by email at Jack@JBleibergCPA.com; www.JBleibergCPA.com.

*Meet
Sean Carroll*

Sean Carroll is a seasoned entrepreneur who is passionate about living life at the highest level and helping others to do the same.

After serving as a public school music teacher for 7 years in New Jersey, Sean chose to step out on his own and start his real estate sales practice in 2004. The only problem with this idea was that he had no sales experience or skills, no real estate experience, and NO CLIENTS. This led Sean straight to financial, emotional, and spiritual bankruptcy and over $140,000 in credit card debt.

Faced with a decision, Sean chose to commit himself to becoming a top Realtor and promised his wife he would "make this work". With the help of some amazing coaches and mentors, he did just that. In just 2 short years, Sean was one of the top producers in his company.

As the real estate market got tougher, Sean's production actually increased, earning him the New Jersey Association of Realtors "Circle of Excellence" sales award in 2008, 2009, and 2010. He grew his business by serving his clients with integrity and passion, and, as a result, nearly 85% of his transactions came via repeat or referral clients.

As his real estate business grew, Sean's colleagues began to seek him out for advice on how to grow their own businesses and he found that he really enjoyed this type of work. He started speaking at local real estate offices and other business events. He noticed that when he was working with others the time just seemed to fly by and he got a real emotional charge from seeing someone else benefit from his knowledge and experience.

Much like he did with his real estate business, Sean attacked the speaking and coaching profession with full force. In less than 2 years, Sean developed an impressive client list, and qualified for full professional membership of the National Speakers Association. In 2012, he was elected to serve on the board of directors for that organization in its New York City chapter.

Sean challenges his clients to take a hard look in the mirror and push themselves beyond what is comfortable to achieve what is possible.

He coaches solo professionals and entrepreneurs to double or even triple their sales without becoming completely overwhelmed by their businesses. After implementing Sean's step-by-step systems, his clients gain clarity, focus, and confidence which enables them to grow their practices but still create the type of lifestyle they want.

Sean strives to have a full life outside of business. He is proud to have recently sung at Carnegie Hall, "zip lined" high above the jungles of Honduras, flown on a trapeze, and run the New York City Half Marathon (and is currently training for the full).

Sean is the author of the chapter *Create a "Get Off Your A$$" Mindset*.

You may reach Sean through the information below:

Sean Carroll
PO Box 645
New York, NY 10156
212-706-7426 – office
908-967-5282 – fax
Sean@SeanCarrollSpeaker.com

*Meet
V. James Castiglia,
Esq.*

Jim Castiglia graduated from Montclair Academy in 1970 and earned his Bachelor of Arts degree from Dickinson College in Carlisle, Pennsylvania in 1974. He also had the privilege of studying for a year at the College's Center for European Studies at the University of Bologna, Italy. He earned his Doctor of Laws degree from Seton Hall University School of Law in 1977. He has been in private practice his entire career, first in West Orange, New Jersey and for the last 19 years in Oak Ridge, New Jersey (Morris County).

Jim's practice focuses on individual, family, and small business legal needs. He is particularly experienced in residential and commercial real estate. He began doing loan modifications before the government's HAMP program was announced and has always processed loan modifications in-house. He helps people in foreclosure by representing them at foreclosure mediation hearings and uses the hearings as a means to obtain a loan modification. In the last several years, a large part of his real estate practice has been mortgage modification negation and foreclosure prevention through mediation hearing as well as the quick disposition of short sales, both for the Buyer and the Seller.

James is the author of the chapter *What Form of Business Should I Set Up?*

You may reach James by the following information:

V. JAMES CASTIGLIA
A Professional Corporation
Counsellor At Law
5701 Berkshire Valley Road
Oak Ridge, NJ 07438
Phone: 973-697-1676
Fax: 973-697-1053
Email: vjc@vjamescastiglia.com

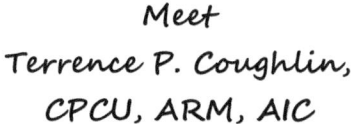

Terrence P. Coughlin is a professional Insurance and Risk Management Consultant with nearly thirty years of finance and insurance experience. He is the principle of Task Risk Management Consulting, Inc., located in Wyckoff, New Jersey. He has held senior positions in the finance and insurance brokerage arenas before spending the last ten years as a Risk Management Consultant.

In addition to his hands-on experience, Terrence has also worked hard on the technical/academic side earning the Charter Property and Casualty Underwriter (CPCU) designation which is the most advanced designation in the insurance industry.

In addition to earning his CPCU, he has also earned his Associate in Risk Management (ARM) and Associate in Claims (AIC) Designations.

Terrence is the author of the chapter *Insurances Every Business Owner Must Have*.

You may contact Terrence by email at coughlin@taskrmc.com.

Meet Rich Dowling, MA, LPC, MAC

Rich Dowling is founder and owner of The Thought Exchange, LLC: Center for Personal Achievement, where he assists others with their desire to create a healthier, happier, more satisfying lifestyle. Rich utilizes The Thought Exchange Process© based largely on the principles of Rational-Emotive Behavior Therapy (REBT) and Cognitive Behavior Therapy (CBT) with the tag line "Change Your Thinking, Enhance Your Life!™".

He is an Adjunct Instructor at Montclair State University and Certified Supervisor at The Albert Ellis Institute. As a founding board member of S.M.A.R.T. Recovery Self-Help Network (Self-Management And Recovery Training), Rich assisted with the development of SMART's 4 Point Program.

Rich is the author of the chapter *Psychological Tips for the Entrepreneur to Stay the Course Through Tough Times*.

You may contact Rich at tte@thethoughtexchange.biz.

Meet Josh Dill

Josh Dill has 25 years of experience in sales and marketing in the commercial insurance and credit card payment processing industries. Dill became aware of the power of business networking about 10 years ago, and it became his primary method of gaining new accounts. When he realized that there was no formal organization for Jewish professionals to network, he went ahead and created one in 2010 - The Jewish Business Network (JBN) www.jbn-biz.com. JBN has become a recognized name in the networking world, and is currently expanding to new geographic areas. Dill is a graduate of Duke University and resides in Baltimore, MD.

Josh is the author of the chapter *In-Person Business Networking*.

You may reach Josh through the information below:

Josh Dill
Charge Card Systems
Senior Account Manager
400 Curry Avenue
Englewood, NJ 07631
201-568-0999
201-568-6054 Fax
jdill@chargecardsystems.com
www.chargecardsystems.com

Meet Ted Fattoross

Ted Fattoross, Network PLUS Founder and CEO, is a professional national speaker with 18 years of experience leading people on the path of personal growth. He presents over 300 programs to over 250,000 people throughout America each year. From small school districts to corporate giants, from the classroom to the boardroom, Ted Fattoross has the knowledge and experience to lead programs on a wide variety of topics, as well as deliver the keynote address for your meeting, in-service and/or conference. He has been featured on national TV, radio programs, newspapers and provides over 300 programs each year for groups as small as 5 and as large as 5,000. Ted serves the corporate, government and non-profit markets in addition to the educational sector, on topics ranging from sales and customer service to teamwork and leadership. Teamwork, communicating effectively, relationship building, values and ethics are threaded through each program. Ted has been on the advisory board for Fortune 500 companies such as Tenneco and Union Camp.

Ted is the author of the chapter *You Are Not Your Business Card*.

You may contact Ted by email at Tedfattoross@tedspeak.com.

Meet Frank Gallipoli

Mr. Gallipoli is the National Sales Director of Bank Card Systems, Inc. in Rochelle Park, New Jersey.

Mr. Gallipoli, with almost 20 years of experience in the finance industry, joined Bank Card Systems to promote current financial products and cutting edge technologies available within the payment card industry for accepting credit cards. Mr. Gallipoli is also able to offer small business owners access to alternative financing options through his numerous business affiliations and relationships. Frank takes a great deal of pride assisting people both in business and personally. He actively serves in the Meadowlands Chamber of Commerce Small Business Council; New Jersey Chamber of Commerce; and supports the Mid-Bergen Rotary Club, Gift of Life 7490 and Interact Club with his wife and children.

Frank is the co-author of the chapters *Merchant Services: Understanding the Costs and Uses to Getting New Clients* and *Alternative Business Financing: Bridge Your Financial Gap*.

Frank is available for your questions at Frank@bcspos.com or at 800-223-8603 (Office)

Meet
Marc Garbar, Esq.

MARC W. GARBAR, ESQ. received his Bachelor of Science degree in Accounting, *cum laude*, from Long Island University. Mr. Garbar received his Juris Doctorate from Nova Southeastern University School of Law. He is admitted to the bar of the States of New Jersey, New York, and Florida.

Mr. Garbar is a litigator in state and federal courts with a practice focused on employment discrimination, sexual harassment, wrongful termination, restrictive covenant litigation, business law, commercial litigation, securities violations, and contract negotiation on behalf of corporations. He also counsels employers in the negotiation of employment termination agreements and assists employers in the formulation and implementation of employment policies including employee handbooks. He serves as lead attorney for the firm in its capacity as Special Counsel representing the State of New Jersey for Labor Negotiation matters.

Marc is the author of the chapter *Employment Law Facts*.

You may contact Marc at (201) 483-9333; (917) 843-8814 (Mobile); or by email at MGarbar@BertonePiccini.com.

*Meet
Ciro J. Giué*

My Mission Statement: *"Great employees make companies. I help great companies keep and attract great employees by helping them design and implement great employee benefits programs that protect their employees and their families and help protect their bottom line."*

Mr. Giué has spent the past 7 years consulting with individuals, families, business owners, and employers on personal insurance matters and designing effective and affordable employee benefits health and welfare programs. Because of Mr. Giué's background as a CPA in New Jersey, he has experience advising his clients and their employees on designing and implementing sophisticated Group Health and Welfare Plans including: IRC Section 105 Plans, IRC Section 125 Plans, High Deductible Health Plans, Flexible Spending Accounts, Ancillary Group Benefits, and Voluntary Supplement Benefits. Prior to this, Mr. Giué spent 15 years on Wall Street working in various capacities for firms that managed assets for institutions, foundations, and families. His roles on Wall Street included Compliance Officer, Assistant Treasurer of Mutual Funds, and Investment Reporting Manager. Prior to working on Wall Street, Mr. Giué worked as a CPA for the largest CPA firm headquartered in New Jersey.

Qualifications

- MBA – Finance/International Business, New York University, Leonard N. Stern School
- Bachelor of Science – Accounting, Rutgers University
- Life and Health Insurance License – NJ, NY, PA, CT.
- FINRA Series 7 and Series 66 License
- Successful completion of the Long Term Care Planning Master Class
- Certified Public Accountant – License is inactive in New Jersey Associations & Memberships

Community Involvement & Interests
- Recipient of the Boys & Girls Clubs of America Service To Youth Award
- Founding Member – MSO Prosperity Chapter of Business Network International
- Bi-Lingual – English and Italian (Communicable in Spanish)

Ciro is the author of the chapter *Medical Care Discount Plans: An Affordable Alternative to Health Insurance.*

You may reach Ciro through the information below:

Ciro J. Giué, MBA
Chief Protection Officer / Chief Benefits Officer
Kinnelon, New Jersey 07405
(201)694-3742 - cjgiue@aol.com

Meet Marie Griffin

Marie Griffin is a business writer and consultant located in Northern New Jersey approximately 35 miles from New York City.

Marie has been a writer and editor for business-to-business websites and magazines for more than 20 years, most recently on a freelance basis. In addition to writing for print publications and the Web, Marie is a content strategist for marketers, and she conducts qualitative research, puts together programming for business events, and creates social media content on a daily basis.

Marie is available to advise business leaders on content strategy, social media strategy and implementation, and custom content creation. She is also interested in helping businesses develop conference programming and business writing assignments.

Marie is the author of the chapter *How to Use Social Media to Boost Your Business*.

Marie can be contacted at migriffinconsulting@msn.com.

Meet
Harry Herbst

Mr. Herbst is a licensed insurance agent who started in 1975. He started his own Insurance Agency in 2002 working with small business owners in small employee benefits arena. Mr. Herbst is a member of the National Association of Insurance agents and Financial Advisors NAIFA. He is also a member of the National Association of Health Underwriter NAHU and was awarded a membership to the prestigious Million Dollar Round Table (MDRT.) He holds a BA from the City University of New York and an MA from the New School for Social Research.

Mr. Herbst also proudly served his country as a U.S. Navy Veteran. He is also Senior Vice Commander of the Jewish War Veterans and a Trustee of Freehold Jewish Center. Active in the various Networking Associations and Chambers of Commerce.

Harry is the author of the chapter *Life and Health Insurance for the Business Owner*. You may reach Harry through the information below:

HARRY HERBST & ASSOCIATES
Insurance & Financial Planning
708 Ginesi Drive
Suite 206
Morganville, NJ 07751
Ph: (732) 536-5200

*Meet
Ronald Hatcher*

Ron Hatcher has over 30 years of experience in marketing communications. He honed his skills in the media department of major agencies including Grey, McCann, Erickson and NW Ayer (which is now MEC). In 1989, he was recruited to be the Media Director of Burkhardt & Christy where he helped the agency to triple in size. In 1995, he formed his own agency, Munn Rabôt, with three other partners.

In 2008, Ron launched Vantage Point Media, a firm focused on providing businesses with highly strategic, effective, and affordable media planning and buying. Ron's extensive brand experience, prior to founding Vantage Point Media, includes BMW Motorcycles, Goodyear Tires, Coca-Cola, AT&T, Bristol Myers, Revlon, R.J. Reynolds, McDonald's, Bahamas Ministry of Tourism, New York-Presbyterian Hospital, Oppenheimer, Sony, Nintendo, Smirnoff Vodka, Nestle and others.

Ron is the author of the chapter *Practical Marketing for Every Business Budget*.

You may contact Ron at Vantage Point Media, LLC at 845-694-8686; 914-584-5576 (Cell) or by email at r.hatcher@vpm.us.com.

Meet Katherine Woodfield Hermes

Ms. Woodfield Hermes has almost two decades of experience working for pharmaceutical giants. She had been exposed to almost every type of health care insurance sold in America. Ms. Woodfield Hermes had worked with doctors and office managers to help them get paid for their reimbursements, and had a unique view on how the patients' families struggled under the weight of unexpected expenses.

As an independent broker, she is able to evaluate each company for the best medical plan available and additionally offer employees the option to choose benefits on a voluntary basis at no cost to the employer. Ms. Woodfield Hermes able to use my knowledge of how the doctors are paid, the insurance companies pay, and help employees avoid financial hardship.

Katherine is the author of the chapter *Low to No-Cost Benefits to Attract and Retain Employees*.

You may reach Katherine through the information below:

Katherine Woodfield Hermes
kwhermes@verizon.net
Phone: 908-421-5381

Meet James Hyland

James Hyland is a graduate from Seton Hall and Upsala Universities. After an extensive career in corporate America, Jim started ASA Payroll in 1990. He sought to give northern New Jersey small business owners an better alternative to the payroll giants. Mr. Hyland's approach includes highly detailed customer service and always being able to give not just more competitive pricing but also provide extensive knowledge and council on a variety of business topics to assist his clients. Mr. Hyland is an expert on IRS and state payroll issues as well and has many times come to the aid of his clients when he has noticed them making a possibility detrimental business maneuver in how they categorize their employees. He has saved many a small business owner from heavy fines and penalties from the IRS through his quick actions and eye for detail. Many of his clients have noticed and appreciated that if they had stayed with a typical payroll giant they could have been tied up in intrusive and lengthily IRS and state investigations had Mr. Hyland not caught and corrected the innocent mistakes.

James is the author of the chapter *W2 or 1099: The Wrong Choice Can Cost Your Business*.

You may contact James at ASA Payroll at 973-728-0433 or by email at jhyland@asapayroll.com.

Meet Vito Mazza

Vito Mazza holds a BA in English in Secondary Education from New Jersey City University in Jersey City, New Jersey. Upon graduation Vito Mazza started his 28 year career with World Book Education Products. He began this career working in the products division as a part time teacher representative and then worked his way through the management levels to distributor level where he became the President of his own company, called Parental Partners, Inc. Afterwards, Mr. Mazza took all of his experience and moved to a national company in the CASH FLOW Management Industry, where he managed their Manhattan office for five years, and won National Recognition in that role. He now serves as the Cash Flow *faster* Consultant for KINUM, INC., helping business owners and medical/dental practices in New Jersey/New York Metro area with cash flow management issues. He also consults with other Businesses in Sales Training, Recruiting and Customer Service.

Vito Mazza is the author of the chapter *Cash-flow Tips for Your Business*. His contact information is:

VITO MAZZA, President
MAZZA CONSULTANTS, LLC.
Vitom3@gmail.com
800-850-5110; 201-446-4072

KINUM, Inc.
WWW.KINUM.COM
vito.mazza@KINUM.COM

Meet Robert J. McDonnell, MS APM

Robert J. McDonnell, owner and principal of Alliance Mediation Services, has been formally practicing mediation since 2003 and brings to his practice over thirty years of experience in the telecommunication industry, focused primarily on regulatory policy development and issue resolution.

He served as President – New Jersey Association of Professional Mediators (NJAPM), from October 2008 through September 2010. He currently serves on the NJAPM Board as Immediate Past President.

Robert is an Accredited Professional Mediator (APM) and received accreditation from the New Jersey Association of Professional Mediators. His practice includes both civil and family mediation services in New Jersey. He has also been accredited as an Advanced Mediator Practitioner by the Association of Conflict Resolution. Robert was trained in mediation and dispute resolution at Rutgers University where he received a Graduate Certificate in Conflict Management.

Robert is the author of the chapter *Mediation for Business Owners*. You may contact Robert by email at rmcdonnell@alliance-mediation.com.

*Meet
Paul Morris*

Paul Morris holds a BS in Engineering and Math from the City College of New York. Paul finished his 11 years in IT as Systems and Programming Manager for ADP in their Brokerage Services Division. After 15 years in IT sales with such companies as Computer Sciences Corp. and Wang Labs, Paul Morris started and ran his own corporate training enterprise designing and selling state-of-the-art classroom and computer-based training solutions to Fortune 500 companies based on the accelerated learning training paradigm. For more than 35 years, Mr. Morris studied extensively in the fields of human development, behavior, and human potential. Paul now serves the private and business community by utilizing his training and human potential techniques.

Paul Morris is the author of the chapter *General Selling Skills*. You may reach Paul through the information below:

Paul Morris, Principal
Paul Morris Associates, Inc.
paulm@fearlessselling.net
Ph: 914.373.4113
Mobile: 845.893.6173
www.FearlessSelling.net

*Meet
Neil Pinkman*

Neil Pinkman is a Regional Director for Paradigm Associates. Neil specializes in coaching entrepreneurs and small companies focused on brand development and growth.

Neil's passion is helping people become successful both personally and professionally. Over the course of his three plus decades of experience as an entrepreneur, Neil has coached hundreds of people to achieve their goals. The wonderful result of Neil's extensive management, both of individuals and teams, is seeing how people and their organizations have thrived and prospered.

Neil's primary focus is helping individuals and organizations implement strategies to increase business, strengthen reputations, enhance personal development, and to expand into new markets while utilizing their unique creative abilities. Neil's specialty areas include design companies, marine-related industries, and holistic practices.

Neil Pinkman is the author of the chapter *Getting Your Business to Survive Tough Economies*.

You may contact Neil at Paradigm Associates at 908-917-8203 or by email at npinkman@paradigmassociates.us.

*Meet
Donna Price*

Donna Price is a Business Success Coach, Speaker, and Facilitator. Her company, Compass Rose Consulting, specializes in working with business leaders and their teams and with small businesses. Leadership coaching includes working to create powerful strategic plans to build effective and high performing teams and create a workplace culture that is healthy. Small business coaching includes strategic planning, business development, marketing strategies, and operational effectiveness.

Donna Price gets business owners and leaders to move their companies in the directions they want. Participants not only produce a transformational shift in their business thinking and real performance results but they also create great businesses for themselves and their employees. Donna Price is instrumental in helping business owners get out of their own way to create powerful strategies and implement their accelerated success.

Donna Price pulls together her years of work with people in a variety of settings to be an excellent facilitator and trainer in the areas of people dynamics, leadership, and team development. Donna has over 18 years mid and upper level management experience, supervised multiple teams and managers, and grew programs from 750,000 to over 2 million in program operations. Her experience includes developing residential options for people with disabilities and as the director of an experiential outdoor education center and summer camp for underserved urban youth. She has been successful in program development, policy and procedure development, staff training, risk management assessment and planning, and program certification and accreditation. She has worked to guide programs to be sustainable for workplaces to be life nurturing and enriching. She has extensive experience facilitating team building programs for both youth and adults using adventure-based activities such as high and low rope courses.

As a Best Year Yet™ Partner, Compass Rose Consulting provides a simple and highly effective strategic planning solution for individuals, small businesses, and teams. It is also effective as a performance improvement appraisal tool.

Donna Price is the co-founder of the Real World Leadership Institute and creator of the small business success system: Bizology Biz. Highly creative, Donna Price is an implementer - getting new ideas and strategies off the ground fast.

Donna Price is the author of the chapters *Vision, Leadership, and Strategy: Along the Path to Building Your Business Success* as well as *Should You Throw In The Towel? Evaluate Current Status, Growth History, and Growth Potential*

You may reach Donna through the information below:

Donna Price
931 Maple Ave, Newton, NJ 07860
Ph: 973-948-7673
dprice@compassroseconsulting.com
www.compassroseconsulting.com
www.bizology.biz

*Meet
Eric B. Segal*

Security Business Solutions, founded by Eric B. Segal in 2002, takes a comprehensive approach to workplace security by evaluating and assessing hiring practices, potential vendor relationships, management, and operating practices. Additionally, Security Business Solutions works closely with Venture Capital Firms, Law Firms, and Accounting Firms in providing their clients with a greater in-depth knowledge of potential business relations and decisions.

In January 2008, the Gateway Regional Chamber of Commerce in Union County honored Security Business Solutions as its "Small Business of the Year".

Recently, Eric B. Segal created and currently teaches a course called "MarketSelf" which assists individuals to maximize their chances of finding employment in today's economy.

Eric B. Segal was President and Chief Operating Officer of Kenzer Corporation, an executive search firm responsible for five branch offices throughout the U.S., and served as the United States Representative Member to INAC (International Network of Associated Consultants) representing 24 countries. During his tenure at Kenzer he was involved in the placement of over 15,000 executives and the volume escalated from $130,000 in 1974 to $22 million in 2000. Kenzer was listed as the twelfth largest search firm in the United States.

Earlier in his career he held positions as Regional Manager of Personnel and Operations at JM Fields; Vice President of Operations at Marshals, and Regional Operations Director at Zayre Corporation.

He received a BS in Business with a major in Industrial Psychology from Boston University.

Eric B. Segal is currently the Treasurer of Camp Loyaltown, Inc, a summer camp for retarded children and adults. He previously served as President of Camp Loyaltown, Inc. for 10 years. He is on the Board of Directors for the AHRC's Nassau Chapter (Association for the Help of Retarded Children). Additionally, he serves as the Co-Chairman of the American Cancer Society's Bergen County Golf Tournament, the largest single-day golf fundraiser for the American Cancer Society. He is also a past recipient of the "Excalibur Award".

Eric B. Segal is the author of the chapter *Background Investigations*. You can contact Eric at:

Security Business Solutions
560 Sylvan Ave
Englewood Cliffs, NJ 07632
Ph: (201) 569-0093
Cell: (201) 874-1478
Fax: 201-569-2717
Eric@securitybusinesssolutions.com
www.securitybusinesssolutions.com

Meet Marlene J. Waldock

Marlene J. Waldock owns 1st Impression Communications, a results-directed communication strategies and solutions company with a focus on communication and presentation skills, founded in 1987. A nationally published writer and seasoned public speaker, for five years she was the host of a weekly TV program, New Jersey Business seen on News 12 New Jersey reaching 1.7 million households in the state. In 2003, she was awarded The Small Business Administration (SBA) Journalist of the Year Award for her work. From 2006 to 2009 as a member of the Board of Contributors for NJBIZ, a weekly business publication, she wrote quarterly editorials on topics pertinent to the business community. She has also authored articles in the Family Circle Magazine on Powerful Communication Skills for Women reaching 22 million readers world-wide.

Perhaps her greatest accomplishment, professionally and personally, is the creation in and the ultimate success of "Because We Are Women": Celebrating Possibilities Symposium. BWAW is an empowering experience that energizes, inspires, and supports personal growth, life achievement, and internal fulfillment. Since 2004, BWAW has touched hundreds of women helping them to step into their own power and live their dreams. In 1995, she became a member of The New Jersey Association of Women Business Owners (NJAWBO) and served as state president in 2003/2004. Just prior to becoming president, the Association honored her when they selected her BUSINESS WOMAN OF THE YEAR.

Very involved in the community, she is the President of the North Essex Chamber of Commerce and sits on the Board for Programs for Parents and the Advisory Board for the Turnaround Management Association. For three years, she participated in the PSE&G Supplier Diversity Council promoting the viability of WBE and MBE as suppliers to Corporate America.

Marlene J. Waldock is the author of the chapter *Public Speaking Skills for Business Owners and Sales Professionals*.

You may reach Marlene through the information below:

Marlene J. Waldock
1st Impression Communications
mjw@1stimpressioncom.com
www.1stimpressioncom.com
Ph: 973 498-0046

Meet Helene Strumeyer

Helene specializes in Sales and Leasing of Office and Industrial property in New Jersey. She assists U.S. and International companies expanding in and to New Jersey in search of warehouse and/or office facilities.

Helene is known for her tenacity and problem solving approach which she brings to all of her commercial real estate transactions.

Helene obtained her Master's Degree in International Relations and International Economics from The Johns Hopkins University School of Advanced International Studies (SAIS). She has resided in Switzerland, Italy, and Israel. For over a decade, she worked as an international public relations executive. In that capacity, she counseled: The North American Economic Mission of the Government of Israel, The Government of Iceland, and the Government of the Philippines.

Helene understands the subtleties necessary to navigate in the international arena and has a comfort level with international executives. This was recently demonstrated when one of the largest energy companies in Europe choose Ms. Strumeyer to represent the firm in their search for their first U.S. office/warehouse. Ms. Strumeyer is a member of the International Business Council of the Meadowlands Chamber of Commerce. She has lived in Bergen County and currently resides in Passaic Park, New Jersey.

SPECIALTIES:

Office and Warehouse Leasing and Sales Negotiations
Procurement
Real Estate Assessment
Government Liason

Helene Strumeyer is the author of the chapter *Tips in Renting or Buying Commercial Real Estate.*

You may reach Helene by email at hstrumeyer@optonline.net.

*Meet
Arnold Rintzler,
Certified Business
Coach*

"People make the difference," says Arnold Rintzler. "More than any other business variable the development of human resources is the key to greater growth and profits." Arnold Rintzler knows his subject. He has successfully coached more than 300 individuals in 40 industries helping them to achieve inspired leadership, employee cohesion, and, ultimately, greater profit. As a Certified Facilitator for the Total Quality Institute and Resources Associates Corporation, he has helped his clients implement "total quality management", a holistic approach to continuous business improvement.

Prior to founding AWR Business Concepts in 1993, Mr. Rintzler spent 29 years in business including 12 years as President of The Casual Woman, a chain of women's apparel stores, which he founded, grew successfully, and sold to a national retailer. He was also a Senior Manager for R.H. Macy Company and Federated Department Stores. He is particularly adept in buying, merchandising, operations, and human resources. Mr. Rintzler started AWR Business Concepts because he knows from experience that "people will willingly accomplish great things given the right support, the right tools, and the right kind of leadership".

As a business consultant, he has worked in manufacturing, construction, and retail as well as professional and service industries. He helps clients with management issues, process improvement, and strategic direction. He has facilitated the development of strategic business and marketing plans plus leadership, sales performance, and employee evaluation.

Mr. Rintzler holds a degree in Psychology from the University of Pittsburgh. His professional certifications include Achievement Seminars International (training and marketing) and the Resource Associate Network (affiliate and trainer). His articles have appeared in newspapers and business publications; he has been featured on radio and TV, and he has been a speaker for many business and professional groups. In addition, Mr. Rintzler is an Adjunct Instructor at Essex County Community College and has taught at the Community College of Morris and The Institute for Business and Professional Development at Kean University.

"Most people have a great deal of potential they are just not using," says Arnold Rintzler. "We help people discover, expand, and develop the skills and attitudes necessary to achieve a higher degree of success both personally and professionally".

Together we work on executing the plans we created. Often, most importantly, we generate greater cash flow that continues the growth trend.

Specialties: Trusted Advisor | Executive Coach | Entrepreneurial Consultant | Business Growth Expert | Assessment Tools | Leadership Development | Sales Development | One Page Strategic Plan

Arnold Rintzler is the author of *Goal Setting: Obtain Your Business Objectives*.

You may reach Arnold at:

Arnold@awrintzler.com
www.awrbusinessconcepts.com
Ph: 973-763-7911

Meet Douglas A. Goldstein, Esq.

Douglas A. Goldstein, Esq. is a shareholder with Spector & Ehrenworth, P.C., a business and bankruptcy boutique law firm based in Florham Park, New Jersey. Douglas A. Goldstein has been practicing law with Spector & Ehrenworth, P.C. since 2002.

Douglas has in-depth experience in a wide range of legal matters ranging from commercial and consumer bankruptcy to business litigation and creditor/debtor rights. He focuses on understanding the client's problem and reaching outside the obvious to find a better solution.

From 2006 through 2013, Douglas has been selected annually in New Jersey Monthly as a Super Lawyers "Rising Star" in the fields of Bankruptcy Law and Creditor and Debtor Rights. Each year, only 2.5 percent of New Jersey attorneys receive "Rising Star" status. "Rising Stars" are determined through a competitive evaluation of attorneys either in practice for 10 years or less or 40 years old or younger.(1)

EDUCATION:

The George Washington University Law School, J.D., 1998;

Cornell University, B.S., 1995

BAR ADMISSIONS:

New Jersey, New York, Maryland, District of Columbia, Supreme Court of the United States, United States Court of Appeals for the Second Circuit, United States District Courts for the District of New Jersey, Southern and Eastern Districts of New York, District of Maryland, and District of Columbia.

(1) No aspect of this advertisement has been approved by the Supreme Court of New Jersey.

Douglas A. Goldstein, Esq. is the author of *Getting Paid Promptly in The Construction Business; New Jersey's Consumer Fraud Act: What is a Consumer?;* and *Being Preferred is Not Always a Good Thing.*

Douglas can be contacted at:

Spector & Ehrenworth, P.C.
30 Columbia Turnpike, Suite 202
Florham Park, NJ 07932
Ph: 973-593-4800 x117
Fax: 973-593-4848

Meet
Brian T. Cody, CFP

Brian T. Cody, CFP, is a Financial Advisor with LPL Financial. Brian T. Cody specializes in all phases of financial planning with an emphasis on retirement planning for small businesses and individuals. His practice is located out of Florham Park, NJ.

Brian T. Cody graduated from the United States Merchant Marine Academy in Kings Point, NY and has a Master's Degree from Union College in Schenectady, NY. He is fully-registered for securities and licensed for insurance services.

Brian is also licensed by the State of New Jersey to provide Continuing Education to Certified Public Accountants.

Brian provides financial presentations to groups around the New Jersey/New York area and is an Adjunct Professor at Fairleigh Dickinson University in Madison, NJ.

A little known fact about Brian is that after graduating from the U.S. Merchant Marine Academy he became a U.S. Navy Nuclear Engineer and trained Navy officers to become licensed nuclear engineers.

Brian T. Cody is the author of *7 Techniques Employers Can Employ to Keep Employees Happy and 3 Attributes Your Next Financial Advisor Must Have*.

Brian can be contacted at:

LPL Financial*
30 Vreeland Road, Building A
Suite 120
Florham Park, NJ 07932
brian.cody@lpl.com
Ph: 973-867-1345
Fax: 973-490-6429

*Member of FINRA/SIPC

Raffi Jamgotchian got his first computer at the age of seven when his dad brought home a Texas Instruments TI-99. Raffi spent many hours programming the external speech synthesizer with random robotic sounding phrases. Later, a large CP/M machine found its way to the garage where Raffi learned to code in BASIC. Fortunately, an Apple II entered his life with a Microsoft CP/M card in it so you could dual boot either CPM or Apple's ProDOS. Raffi's uncle then bought a C compiler for Raffi which then began his learning experience there.

In junior high school, Raffi began exploring Bulletin Board Systems (BBS) in the mid-80s and ran one with a few of his friends for a couple of years. Although he found out that being a computer nerd in the late 80s in high school was not in style, Raffi continued to pursue his hobbies.

In 1993, Raffi Jamgotchian graduated with a BS in Computer and Systems Engineering from Rensselaer Polytechnic Institute and began working with Crestron Electronics as a Systems Engineer programming custom control systems for board rooms, conference centers, medical facilities, and arenas. His work in this area led him in 1995 to Chancellor Capital Management which was later purchased by INVESCO. Initially working as a help-desk technician and overnight job scripter, Raffi went on to become the Help Desk Manager and later the Director of IT Infrastructure for New York. In 2006, Raffi left INVESCO to help start a boutique investment firm, Canaras Capital Management, and, in 2008, left to start Triada Networks.

Raffi Jamgotchian is the author of *Risk Awareness*. Raffi can be contacted at:

Raffi Jamgotchian
President/CTO
Triada Networks
Raffi@triadanet.com
www.triadanet.com
Ph: 201-297-7778

Meet Julbert J. Abraham

Julbert J. Abraham has 10 years of experience in marketing, sales, and entrepreneurship. Julbert J. Abraham is the CEO of Abraham Global Services, LLC and the Managing Partner of Abraham Global Marketing (AGM). AGM is a marketing boutique located in the Greater New York City area with a focus on LinkedIn Marketing. AGM provides Educational Webinars, Workshops, Courses, and Seminars where we teach our clients how to leverage LinkedIn to grow their business. In addition, we provide Account Management Services where we support our clients' LinkedIn accounts.

Julbert comes from a humble beginning being born and raised in Port-au-Prince, Haiti. He came to the U.S. at an early age where he received a Bachelor Degree in Marketing at Cheyney University in Pennsylvania then his MBA at Northeastern University in Boston, Massachusetts. In his spare time, he enjoys traveling, cooking, networking, and giving back to his community by mentoring the youth and volunteering with local non-profits.

Julbert J. Abraham is the author of *Five LinkedIn Tricks to Double Your Sales*. Julbert can be reached at 862-253-1837.

Notes: _____

www.ingramcontent.com/pod-product-compliance
Lightning Source LLC
Chambersburg PA
CBHW060500090426
42735CB00011B/2058